ISBN 978-1-330-87405-9
PIBN 10071580

1 MONTH OF
FREE
READING

at

www.ForgottenBooks.com

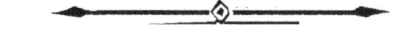

By purchasing this book you are eligible for one month membership to ForgottenBooks.com, giving you unlimited access to our entire collection of over 1,000,000 titles via our web site and mobile apps.

To claim your free month visit:

www.forgottenbooks.com/free71580

English
Français
Deutsche
Italiano
Español
Português

www.forgottenbooks.com

Mythology Photography **Fiction**
Fishing Christianity **Art** Cooking
Essays Buddhism Freemasonry
Medicine **Biology** Music **Ancient**
Egypt Evolution Carpentry Physics
Dance Geology **Mathematics** Fitness
Shakespeare **Folklore** Yoga Marketing
Confidence Immortality Biographies
Poetry **Psychology** Witchcraft
Electronics Chemistry History **Law**
Accounting **Philosophy** Anthropology
Alchemy Drama Quantum Mechanics
Atheism Sexual Health **Ancient History**
Entrepreneurship Languages Sport
Paleontology Needlework Islam
Metaphysics Investment Archaeology
Parenting Statistics Criminology
Motivational

MANUAL OF AGRICULTURE

FOR SECONDARY SCHOOLS

STUDIES IN SOILS AND CROP PRODUCTION

BY

D. O. BARTO, B.S.

INSTRUCTOR IN SECONDARY SCHOOL AGRICULTURE
COLLEGE OF AGRICULTURE, UNIVERSITY
OF ILLINOIS

WITH INTRODUCTION BY

E. DAVENPORT, M.Agr., LL.D.

DEAN OF THE COLLEGE OF AGRICULTURE
UNIVERSITY OF ILLINOIS

BOSTON, U.S.A.

D. C. HEATH & CO., PUBLISHERS

1910

agric
Main Lib.

INTRODUCTION

WE are making educational history these days at a rapid rate, and not the least important chapter is on the new status of affairs industrial. At last agriculture is coming into its own, and it will not be many years until this subject will have taken its place in the American secondary school system as it is now taking its place within the colleges and universities.

This is not only because agriculture employs the time and absorbs the lives of a third of our people and feeds us all; it is not only because the future and the development of every people is limited by the production of the soil it occupies; it is not only because it is expedient from the community standpoint that this subject should be studied by young people and developed by science; it is largely because, after all, the subject-matter of agriculture, its method and its outlook, are exceptionally valuable in their influence upon the individual, educationally.

Elsewhere[1] I have written, "It is dangerous to attempt to educate a live boy with no reference to the vocational," and I might add that it is dangerous to the community, as it is unprofitable to the individuals, to fill our schoolhouses day after day with young men and women to study seriously all the problems of life except the one supreme problem of how to make a living, a large and significant portion of which problem from the racial standpoint is comprised within the range of farming and farm life.

The introduction of agriculture into the secondary schools has been delayed from the same causes which have retarded the devel-

[1] "Education for Efficiency," Chapter I, Heath & Co., 1909.

iii

opment of the agricultural colleges ; viz., want of teachers, ignorance of suitable matter and methods, and the lack of an adequate literature both for reference and for text.

It has taken the colleges more than forty years to overcome, even measurably, this inherent handicap upon a new academic subject, rendered more serious in this case because of peculiar ancient traditions regarding the ideals and the scope of education. In the last five years, however, the future of these colleges has not only become assured, but their success has engendered the demand that agriculture be also taught in schools other than colleges, not only to relieve congestion there, but more especially to bring to the masses of people where it will do the utmost possible good the recent findings of science regarding the maintenance of the food supply of a people, on the one hand, and that standard of life and living that find their highest exemplification in a properly developed country life.

The next place for agriculture, therefore, is in the secondary schools, and their period of trial ought to be far more brief than that of the colleges. This is because, though teachers are yet to be produced, the colleges, in their experience, have learned much, both of matter and of method, that can be transferred directly into the secondary school, particularly the well-organized high school with a country constituency. These same colleges, too, in coöperation with the normal schools, are able to produce, and are already producing, eminently qualified teachers.

From now on the supply of teachers will come along in natural response to a demand that takes all promising candidates at maximum salaries, so that the great business of the immediate future, and one that must largely be left to the enterprise of individuals and the initiative of far-seeing publishers, is the production of suitable reference and text-books, for no subject is teachable till it has an adequate literature.

These books are now springing up, as if by magic, from all sorts of unexpected places. The surprising fact is that there are so many, and the still more surprising fact is that they are so good — better by far, most of them, than the best that were available for college purposes when the writer was a student.

Too many of these books, unfortunately, are confessedly "elementary," whereas it is not elementary agriculture that the farmer most needs. What he wants is instruction in the elementals of agriculture. It is the fundamentals of the subject that need to be emphasized and taught, and fortunately many of these books belie their titles and are not, after all, "elementary," but elemental.

Many of these texts cover the entire range of agriculture, though necessarily in abbreviated treatment. There are those who believe that when agriculture is fully introduced as a secondary school subject, it will consist, as in college, not of one but of several courses, each with its distinctive and separate text. Such a text the author has attempted to produce, dealing with a somewhat restricted and altogether definite field — the soil and the principal crops of the northern states.

Most books heretofore prepared have been repositories of information to be studied and recited like other subjects. This book is distinctively a laboratory manual, the belief of the author being that the student should be led to study agriculture at first hand, and that his impressions as well as his knowledge of the subject should be gained through the most intimate personal contact, remembering always that it is the science of agriculture and not its art or handicraft that is teachable in our schools.

The author is eminently qualified to treat the subject he undertakes. A farmer by instinct, with a long and successful career as a teacher in secondary schools, he took the agricultural course at the University of Illinois in the ripeness of full maturity. He has since that time given his exclusive attention to the adaptation of agriculture to secondary instruction, for which he has enjoyed exceptional advantages through his connection with the agricultural extension department of the university. He therefore brings to this book not only the instincts of a farmer, but the knowledge of the specialist and the ripeness of judgment of a mature and successful teacher.

It is to be hoped that if this attempt shall prove successful, either this author or others equally able and equally willing to perform a labor of love will extend the laboratory manual idea to other fields of this most fascinating subject.

E. DAVENPORT.

PREFACE

THROUGHOUT the country to-day many schools of secondary grade are expressing a desire to add to their present curricula of studies courses of instruction in agriculture; but they are in doubt as to the character and extent of the work which would be possible or advisable for them to offer in this subject.

While a considerable number of elementary books in agriculture has been written in recent years, few, if any, of them were prepared for high school grades, and do not assume to compare in the character of matter presented or in their thoroughness of the treatment of the subject with texts in the other sciences taught in high schools.

Agriculture is now recognized as embracing so large a field, with so many different divisions and special interests, that no single book within the proper bounds of a high school text could pretend to compass the whole subject. The work should be presented in separate courses which may be taken by classes either in the order of their natural sequence, or a selection can be made of those courses most directly related to the particular agricultural interests of the communities where the schools are situated.

There are many excellent books on the various topics included in each department of agriculture, and a great wealth of agricultural information has been published in bulletin form. All of this is available matter for reference and should be of much value to teachers and students in their work; but as yet there are no texts in agriculture that have been prepared to meet the special needs of high school courses. There is no question, however, but that the urgent demand for such texts will call forth in the near future many good books, and in the meantime much may be done with the material now at hand in making a beginning in the work of secondary school agriculture.

The purpose of this Manual is to outline a course of study in agriculture, covering at least one year's work, which shall be of high school grade, and shall offer training in sciences comparable to that furnished by the other science courses in good high schools.

The writer believes that all of the work in agriculture taught in our high schools should be of such character that it will appeal to the practical farmer as *real agriculture*, possible of application to actual conditions and closely related to the affairs of the homes and the farms of the community. In addition to this it should possess such educational value, both in its content and in its opportunities for training in scientific methods and habits, as to justify its place in the curriculum of any good high school.

The work as outlined in this course is confined to studies in soils and crop production. Since the growing of crops is the basis of all farming operations and every form of agriculture is intimately associated with the cultivation of the soil, it seems best to make this work the foundation for the courses in agriculture to be taught in high schools.

Then, following this, a study of the breeds and types of the most important farm animals and something of the laws of breeding and improvement of stock, a study of methods of feeding, the principles of nutrition and a comparison of the nutrient values of the different foodstuffs produced and used on the farm, the symptoms, causes, treatment, and prevention of the more common ailments of domestic animals, the composition and care of milk and the testing of milk for butter fat, a study of the more common insect pests and plant diseases with the proper treatment for each, and the preparation of the different insecticides and fungicides, — such topics as these might be selected as material for the work of a second course.

The plan of work suggested in this Manual includes recitations following the reading and discussion of the portions of texts and bulletins treating each topic as it is taken up combined with exercises in the laboratory and supplemented wherever possible with pot-culture work and field experiments.

Many of the laboratory exercises are the same that are used in the courses in agricultural colleges, for it is believed that the work in high school agriculture should hold the same relation to college agriculture as exists in the case of the other high school sciences, — botany, zoölogy, physics, chemistry, and in mathematics and languages, — with the expectation that many high schools will be able to do work in agriculture for which college credits can be allowed.

In Part I, Exercise 1 is borrowed from *Soil Physics Laboratory Guide* by Professors Stevenson and Schaub of Iowa State College. Exercises 2 to 20 inclusive are taken from *Laboratory Manual for Soil Physics* by Professor J. G. Mosier of the University of Illinois. In a few instances they have been slightly altered to adapt them to the purposes of the book.

In Part II, page 52, acknowledgment is made to Dr. C. G. Hopkins and Professor J. H. Pettit of the University of Illinois for material used.

In the work with corn the author has drawn very freely from the admirable circular, *Studies of Corn and Its Uses*, prepared by Professor Fred H. Rankin of the University of Illinois.

CONTENTS

PART I. STUDIES ABOUT SOILS

MANUAL OF AGRICULTURE

PART I. — STUDIES ABOUT SOILS

I. — Physical Composition of the Soil

"THE soil is not a mere inert mixture. Its parts have shape and size and arrangement, as well as being merely composed of certain substances. All of these parts have been separately formed, moved, and assorted, and then laid down together as we find them; and, moreover, they are not even yet at rest, but are always taking new forms and new places and making new partnerships, entailing a never-ending series of mysteries. From the soil all things come; and into it all things at last return; and yet it is always new and fresh and clean, and always ready for new generations. This soft, thin crust of the earth — so infinitesimally thin that it cannot be shown in proper scale on any globe or chart — supports all of the countless myriads of men and animals and plants, and has supported them for countless cycles, and will continue to yet support for other countless cycles. In view of all this achievement, it is not strange that we do not yet know the soil and understand it; and we are in mood to be patient with our shortcomings." — BAILEY, *Cyclopedia of American Agriculture.*

The soil, in an agricultural sense, is always a *mixture* of inorganic and organic matter. If either of these materials be lacking, it is not a true soil. The organic matter is composed of bits of decaying plant or animal substances — usually both. Disintegrated and pulverized rock constitute the inorganic portion of the soil. Soil particles differ in size, form, and arrangement, in weight and color. In most cultivated soils the inorganic material forms from 85 per cent to 95 per cent by weight of the mass. A sandy soil is usually deficient in organic matter, while peaty soils contain an excess of it.

The object of Exercise 1 is to help the student to get a correct conception of the physical composition of some of the common types of soil.

REFERENCES: King, *The Soil*, pp. 27–76. Fletcher, *Soils*, pp. 3–27, 46–74. Snyder, *Soils and Fertilizers*, pp. 9–56. Warington, *Physical Properties of Soil*, pp. 1–50.

EXERCISE 1

Examination of Soil Particles with Microscope

I. — Place upon a glass slide a few grains of coarse sand and examine carefully with the low power of the microscope, noting these points : —

    (*a*) Color — white, gray, brown, red, or black.
    (*b*) Shape — angular, rounded, or irregular.
    (*c*) Simple or compound grains.
    (*d*) Size — coarse, medium, or fine.

II. — In the same way study other types of soils — fine sand, loam, silt, clay, loess, and peat.

On separate sheets make drawings of a number of particles of each kind of soil, and describe them with reference to (a), (b), (c), and (d).

II. — Moisture Relations of Soils

The study of the moisture relations of soils as affected by differences in their physical constitution, or by differences in their texture due to the character of the cultivation which they have received, is probably the largest and most interesting problem in soil physics.

The capacity of a soil to absorb water in large amounts, to hold it in a·form that does not prevent the free development of the roots of plants to a sufficient depth, and the ability to lift this water from below, as the needs of the growing crops demand it, up into the zone occupied by their roots, are the ideal conditions of the soil which the skillful farmer tries to secure. The study of soil physics is to help him understand the principles which control these conditions.

In Exercise 2 the objects are: —

(1) To show that the moisture content of a soil depends in part upon its surface conditions, *i.e.* what demands the crop growing on it is making for water, and what the character is of the surface cultivation.

(2) To determine the relative amounts of water stored in the ground at different depths, — in strata commonly designated as *surface*, *subsurface*, and *subsoil*.

The determination of the moisture content of a soil is a very simple process, and its frequent use on the farm would pay for the trouble it costs. In this way one may easily test the difference in the amounts of water in the ground at different depths due to fall *versus* spring plowing, to early *versus* late spring plowing, to differences resulting from various kinds of surface cultivation and surface mulching, etc.

All of the work should be done carefully and accurately in every exercise. Otherwise it has absolutely no value in results obtained and, besides, is very bad training.

REFERENCES: King, *The Soil*, pp. 154–170. Fletcher, *Soils*, pp. 75–84. Snyder, *Soils and Fertilizers*, pp. 22–25. Warington, *Physical Properties of Soil*, pp. 51–57, 64–73.

EXERCISE 2

Determination of Total Moisture in Samples of Field Soils

According to directions given below,[1] collect samples of soils from (1) an old sod, (2) between the rows of corn, (3) tilled ground where no crop is growing. Take the samples in each case from the surface, subsurface, and subsoil.

[1] Directions for collecting soil samples: For this purpose a one-and a-half or two-inch auger, with an extension making it 40 inches long, is used. In collecting samples for moisture determinations, expose the soil as little as possible to the air before putting in jars. Collect the surface soil to the depth of the plow line, usually about 7 inches. After this part of the sample is removed, the hole is enlarged sufficiently so that the subsurface soil may be taken without coming in contact with the surface soil. Take the subsurface sample to the subsoil line as indi-

Mark and carefully weigh six soil pans. Run all experiments in duplicates for the sake of greater accuracy.

Place in each soil pan 100 grains of the soil sample to be studied, taking the weights rapidly to prevent loss by evaporation. Put them in the drying oven for five hours at a temperature of 100° to 110° C. Cool to room temperature and weigh at once. The loss in weight represents the total moisture content of the soil.

If three students work together, one might take the surface, another the subsurface, and the third the subsoil. Then compare results.

Tabulate the results as follows : —

Total Moisture Determination

Kind of Soil.	Pan No.	Wt. of Pan.	Wt. of Soil.	Wt. of Soil and Pan.	Wt. of Dry Soil and Pan.	Wt. of Dry Soil.	Loss of Wt.	Per Cent Moisture.

cated by the change in color, texture, and physical composition. Commonly this line is found at a depth of 16 to 20 inches. Enlarge and clean out the hole as before. Since the change from subsurface to subsoil is not a sharp line, but usually somewhat gradual, we discard about two inches of the intermediate mixture. The subsoil is then collected to a depth of 40 inches, if possible.

In some soils the subsurface layer may be absent, the subsoil being reached by the plow, while in others, as in peaty and sandy soils, no true subsoil may be found within 40 inches of the surface. In such cases only two samples are taken.

State the weather conditions when the samples were collected and the amount of the rainfall during the previous week.

Which soil had largest water content? Which had the least? What is the explanation? Was most water found in the surface, subsurface, or subsoil?

III. — Different Forms of Soil Moisture

Most of the water in the soil comes from the rains and snows that fall on the surface of the ground. A part of what falls is quickly evaporated before it soaks into the ground. Another portion forms into rills and flows over the surface joining larger streams and usually carrying in its currents more or less of the richest particles of the soil, to be eventually lost in the sea. The amount of water, with its burden of soil, that is thus lost to the farmer depends largely upon the topography of the land and the condition of its surface. In a hilly country, and wherever the upper soil is packed and bare of vegetation, the surface wash is likely to be serious.

The remaining part of the rainfall and melting snows gradually sinks into the ground, and is either absorbed by the soil particles and held as a film over their surfaces, or it percolates down through the cracks and crevices in the soil, obeying the law of gravity, until it reaches the level of standing water, commonly spoken of as the *water table*.

Of all these divisions of the water which comes to the earth as rain and snow, it is only the portion that soaks into the ground and is held as *film water* around the soil particles which is directly concerned in supplying growing plants with moisture, and for this reason is of greatest interest to the agriculturist. This moisture is called *capillary moisture* because it moves in all directions through the interstices between the soil particles by the force of capillary attraction, just as oil in a lamp flows upward through the wick.

But not all of the film water about the soil grains is free to move under the influence of capillary attraction. Adhering to the surfaces of all solids of atmospheric temperature is an exceedingly thin film of moisture which can be expelled only by exposure to a high degree of heat. This film of water is known as *hygroscopic moisture*, and can.be driven off from the soils only by keeping them in a drying oven at a temperature of about 105° C. for five or six hours. Roots of plants are unable to overcome the adhesive power which holds this film of moisture to the soil particles. On the other hand, the greater part of the layer of moisture surrounding the soil grains is held so loosely that the plant roots can absorb it readily by a force called *osmosis*, and when exposed to the air it is carried off by evaporation.

In Exercise 2 the *total* moisture content of the soil was determined by using the drying oven and expelling both the capillary and the hygroscopic moisture at the same time. The residue remaining in the soil pans is *water-free* soil, and this is taken as the basis in all computations and data relating to soils, because it is the only uniform condition that can be secured.

In Exercise 3 only a determination of the capillary moisture is sought, and this requires merely an exposure of the soils to the air until a constant weight is reached, that is, until all the capillary moisture has evaporated.

REFERENCES: King, *The Soil*, pp. 173–178. Fletcher, *Soils*, pp. 29–31, 87–90. Warington, *Physical Properties of Soil*, pp. 92–107.

EXERCISE 3

Determination of Capillary Moisture in Field Soils

Use soils from the same samples taken for Exercise 2. (The jars should be kept tightly sealed except when the samples are being weighed out. Mix the soils well by thoroughly shaking the jars before opening.)

Number and weigh carefully 6 soil pans. Place in each 100 grams of soil, running duplicates of surface, subsurface, and subsoil. With a glass rod carefully break up all lumps and spread the soil evenly over bottom of . pan. Let the soils dry at room temperature, and take the weights every 24 hours. When the weight becomes constant, the loss indicates the amount of capillary moisture.

Compute the percentage of capillary moisture in each sample on the basis of the water-free soil as found in Exercise 2. Tabulate the results as in the previous exercise.

Notice that the difference between the *total* moisture content and the amount of capillary moisture in a sample represents approximately the hygroscopic moisture of that soil.

How does this compare in amount with the per cent of capillary moisture?

Are the amounts about the same for all of the soils and in the same relative order for surface, subsurface, and subsoil?

IV. — Soil Temperature and its Control

A warm soil is superior to one that is cold for crop production. For each kind of crop there is a minimum temperature below which its seeds will not germinate. There is also for every kind of plant an optimum temperature for growth. A plant produced from a seed that has germinated in a soil too cold for the plant to start with a vigorous growth becomes stunted and never reaches maximum development. The various forms of microörganisms and chemical processes in the soil, upon whose activities the fertility of soils is largely dependent, require a warm environment for their best work.

The gain of a few days at the beginning of the season, for many crops, constitutes a large factor in their success.

Most farmers do not realize that soil temperature is a thing over which they may have much control, and probably a majority of them would think that the difference of a few degrees is of too little consequence to be considered. But the scientist, the engineer, the professional man, the manufacturer, and the business man have all been trained to appreciate the importance of every factor that enters into their work. It is here that the training of the farmer has been especially weak; and it is the province of the study of the science of agriculture to correct this fault in his training and teach him how he may control conditions which before he had supposed were beyond his power to influence.

An undrained or wet soil is cooler than a dry one,

because there is so much greater evaporation of moisture from its surface, and the amount of heat required
to vaporize a pound of water is very considerable. It
requires four or five times as many heat units to raise
a given weight of water 1° F. as are needed for the
same amount of dry soil. The object in Exercise 4 is
to demonstrate and impress these facts.

REFERENCES : King, *The Soil*, pp. 218–227, 234–238. Fletcher,
Soils, pp. 33–34. Warington, *Physical Properties of Soil*, pp. 165–178.

EXERCISE 4

Effect of Drainage on Soil Temperature

Make two wooden boxes 3 × 4 feet and 6 inches deep, building
one water-tight and the other loose enough to allow the water to
drain off. Fill each box with the same kind of soil, and apply the
same amounts of water till drainage begins in the loose box. The
boxes should stand in the open air, where evaporation is free. After
drainage has ceased, take the temperature of the soils in each box
hourly, on a clear day, at the depths of 1, 2, and 4 inches.

Give explanations for the differences in temperature.

Why is clay called a cold soil, and sand warm?

V. — Influence and Control of Color of Soils

The color of the surface soil has a marked influence
on its temperature. Between soils of dark color and
those of a light hue there is often found a difference of
5° to 10° F. at a depth of 2 to 5 inches. For many crops
early in the season this is a matter of considerable importance. Soils containing large amounts of organic

matter are dark colored. Through careless or unwise cultivation, soils gradually grow lighter colored. The farmer's control of these conditions comes mainly through the use of barnyard manure and the plowing under of green crops. In Exercise 5 there is an opportunity to demonstrate two things : —

(1) Dark-colored soils absorb a larger proportion of heat from the rays of the sun than do light-colored soils.

(2) Seeds will germinate more quickly and plants grow more rapidly in soils of dark color than in those of light color.

REFERENCES : King, *The Soil*, p. 230. Fletcher, *Soils*, pp. 34–36. Warington, *Physical Properties of Soil*, pp. 161–164.

EXERCISE 5

Effect of Color of Soil on Temperature

Fill a wooden tray 6 feet long, 3 feet wide, and 6 inches deep with well pulverized soil of a light color. By a wire drawn taut across the tray lengthwise, divide the surface into halves. Then, by other lines drawn crosswise of the tray, divide each half into 6 equal plots. Designate the corresponding plots in each half by the same letter, and in each two plots, similarly marked, plant the same kind and number of seeds, using corn, peas, beans, oats, wheat, and rye. In one half of the tray bury the seeds $\frac{3}{4}$ inch deep in the soil; in the other half cover them with $\frac{1}{2}$ inch of the light-colored earth,[1] and then add $\frac{1}{4}$ inch of some dark soil or of soot, so that the seeds in every plot are covered to the same depth.

[1] If it is not easy to obtain a soil that is quite light or quite dark in color, the soil in half of the tray can be whitened by a thin dressing of lime or chalk dust, and the other half darkened by soot.

(*a*) Every morning and evening observe the number of plants showing above the surface on each plot and carefully record them, comparing results in the light-colored soil with those in the dark earth.

(*b*) Choose a clear day and make observations of the temperatures of the soils in the two halves of the tray.   Insert thermometers in the soil to the depths of 1, 2, and 4 inches in both the light-colored earth and the dark-colored earth, and take hourly readings from 7 A.M. to 5 P.M.   Keep all parts of the tray equally moist.

Each student may look after the planting of a single plot, but he must make observations on all plots in the tray and hand them in in tabular form.

Which tray shows the higher temperature?   Why?

Why can you see the corn rows on the low, black land sooner after planting than upon the higher, light-colored soil?

VI. — Effect of Lime on Heavy Soils

One of the most difficult problems that many farmers have to deal with in the cultivation of their land is how to handle their clay soils and fine silts so that the proper texture of the soil shall be preserved.

A peculiarity of these soils if they are stirred when too moist, is that they become pasty and run together so that on drying they are hard like cement.   This quality is due to the fineness of the soil grains, which are so small that if they are packed closely together the interstices between them are not large enough for either water or air to penetrate.   When a soil is in this condition, it is of little value for farming purposes.   A soil is said to be in *good tilth* when the individual soil grains are massed together in *crumbs* or *granules* about the size of timothy seed. Now it has been discovered that the action of lime upon a clay soil is to cause the fine particles to flocculate and assume a crumbly texture, making the soil lighter to till and more easily drained.

The object in Exercise 6 is to demonstrate to the student the possibility of controlling the conditions of texture in fine-grained soils by the application of lime.

REFERENCES : King, *The Soil*, p. 30. Warington, *Physical Properties of Soils*, pp. 30–33.

EXERCISE 6

Determination of the Effects of Lime on Plastic Soils

Two students may work together in this experiment.

Weigh out six 300-gram samples of the clay soil, using them as follows : to sample

No. 1, check, add no lime.

No. 2, add .5 gram of air-slacked lime.

No. 3, add 1 gram of air-slacked lime.

No. 4, add 5 grams of air-slacked lime.

No. 5, add 10 grams of air-slacked lime.

No. 6, add 10 grams sand.

Mix each sample thoroughly in a soil pan with the lime, and add just enough water to make plastic.

Fill the semicircular molds,[1] first placing in each a damp, thin

---

[1] It may be easier to make molds with dimensions $4'' \times 2'' \times 1''$.

The test can be made by suspending from the middle of the stick a bucket into which sand is slowly poured until the weight is secured which is necessary to break the stick.

cloth to facilitate the removal of the clay.   Make duplicates of each sample, being careful to compress each to the same degree.   Place on a cloth in a soil pan and dry in an oven for five hours at 105° C.

Test the strength of each brick by supporting the ends so as to allow just three inches between points of support.   Hang a weight pan in middle of the brick, and determine the weight necessary to break each one.

Express data in tabular form.

Explain the effect of lime.

Why does the sand not have as much effect as the lime on the breaking strength ?

EXERCISE 7

Weight of Soils

Determine the cubic contents of a box the three dimensions of which are from 6 to 12 inches.   Take the weight of the box and contents when filled with different air-dry soils, *viz.* sand, clay, loam, loess, and peaty soil.   In filling the box, do not compact the soil.   From the data obtained, compute the weight per cubic foot of each soil.

Calculate the weight of an acre of each soil to the usual depth of the plow line, 7 inches.

The weight of a cubic foot of water is 62.42 pounds.   The *apparent* specific gravity of each soil tested may be found as follows :—

$$\frac{Volume\ wt.\ of\ soil}{Volume\ wt.\ of\ water} = apparent\ specific\ gravity\ of\ soil.$$

In this computation the *water-free* weight of the soil should be used.   To do this, determine the per cent of hygroscopic moisture in a small sample of this soil.   The weight of any given volume of this soil divided by one plus the rate per cent of the moisture, will give as a quotient the weight of water-free soil.

EXERCISE 8

Determination of the Apparent Specific Gravity of Surface Soil under Field Conditions

Take a tube provided for the purpose, and force it into the ground to the depth of six inches. Remove soil to a weighed pan, and dry in the oven at 105° C. for at least ten hours. Find weight of volume of water equal to that of the soil taken, and divide the weight of the water-free soil by this. The result will be the apparent specific gravity.

The apparent specific gravity of soils in the field may be taken as an approximate indication of the tilth of the soils, since the better the tilth the less will be the apparent specific gravity for the same kind of soil. This is due to the fact that soils in good tilth are looser on account of the presence of organic matter and better granulation. The apparent specific gravity of a continuously cropped soil is higher than one having proper rotations. Why?

What would be the approximate weight of a cubic foot of soil under the above conditions?

EXERCISE 9

Determination of the Weight of Soil per Acre-foot

Drive into the soil a brass tube (8″ long and about 3″ in diameter, sharpened at its lower edge) until the top is level with the surface.

Dig away the soil around the tube; empty the tube upon a piece of oilcloth and transfer the soil to a Mason jar; carefully drive the tube down again, and thus obtain a sample of the succeeding eight inches. Repeat this operation until eight-inch samples of the soil have been secured to any desired depth. Carefully weigh each sample. Determine the total moisture in 100 grams of soil from each depth, and from these data determine the weight of the water-free soil. Calculate in cubic inches the content of the tube.

Calculate the weight of an acre of soil to the depth at which each sample was taken. Tabulate the results.

EXERCISE 10

Determination of Specific Gravity of Soils. Volumetric Method

Determine exactly the amount of water required to fill the measuring flask to the 50 cubic centimeter mark by using a burette. Place about 20 grams of soil in the flask and add a measured quantity of distilled water, and shake well to expel the air from the soil.

Fill the flask up to the mark from the burette, and note the total amount of water used, including the hygroscopic water of the soil. This amount, subtracted from the volume of the flask, will give the water displaced by the soil. Calculate the specific gravity and tabulate the results.

Use for this experiment sand, clay, and loam soils.

VII. — Questions concerning the Weight of Soils

If the soil were a solid mass, the determination of its weight would be a simple matter. The specific gravity of the material which forms the great bulk of most soils is about 2.6. Since a cubic foot of water weighs nearly $62\frac{1}{2}$ pounds, a cubic foot of soil, then, would weigh 2.6 times $62\frac{1}{2}$ pounds, or $162\frac{1}{2}$ pounds. (This, of course, refers to the weight of water-free soil.)

But the fact is, a soil is not a solid mass. On the contrary, it is composed of more or less spherical particles which touch each other only at certain points of contact. Nearly 50 per cent of a given volume of cultivated soil is air space. This pore space necessarily reduces the weight of any volume of soil much below the specific gravity of its constituents ; hence, we use the two terms, " real specific gravity " and " apparent specific gravity."

There is a wide variation in the weights of different arable soils, owing to the differences in the amounts of humus in their composition, and in the size of their soil particles. For these reasons surface soils are usually lighter than subsoils. A fertile garden soil weighs about 70 pounds per cubic foot, while an ordinary sandy loam weighs 90 to 95 pounds.

The figures taken for the approximate weight of dry soil on an acre of arable land are 4,000,000 pounds to the depth of 12 inches, and 2,000,000 pounds for the 7 surface inches.

Exercises 7, 8, 9, and 10 are given that the student may have opportunity to verify the statements made by different writers in regard to the weights and specific gravities of soils, and also that he may learn at first hand how soils of different types compare in these respects.

REFERENCES : Fletcher, *Soils*, pp. 26–27. Snyder, *Soils and Fertilizers*, pp. 9–11. Warington, *Physical Properties of Soil*, pp. 41–49.

VIII. — Porosity of Soils

As has been stated in a former paragraph, because the soil mass is made up of rounded particles more or less loosely packed together, there is left between them a considerable space that is occupied by air or water, and is called the *pore space* of the soil. The amount of pore space varies from something over 50 per cent in very fine clay soils to 25 or 30 per cent in coarse sands of uniform texture. It is greatest in the fine-grained soils because these particles, unlike those of sandy soils, are too light to pack closely of their own weight.

Under ordinary field conditions of a cultivated soil, the pore space is increased by the stirring of the ground and the addition of organic matter. It is the pore space of a soil which measures its capacity to hold water. For example, if 50 per cent of the surface foot of a certain soil is pore space, the capacity of that soil to take up water before it is forced to flow away over the surface or to penetrate deeper into the ground is equal to six inches of rainfall.

Moreover, the various forms of living organisms that work in the soil and are essential to its fertility require the presence of air to live and work. Both the oxygen and the nitrogen in the air are needed for the chemical combinations that take place in a fertile soil. The roots of growing plants demand air just as animals do, and when the supply is shut off the plants die.

For all these reasons a fertile soil must have a generous amount of pore space for the circulation of air.

These are important matters in the business of growing crops, and the farmer should thoroughly understand and appreciate them.

Exercise 11 presents two methods for determining the amount of pore space in soils.

REFERENCE: Warington, *Physical Properties of Soil*, pp. 64–73.

EXERCISE 11

Determination of Porosity

FIRST METHOD

Weigh a graduated cylinder.

Use sand, loam, silt, clay, and peat.

Fill to the 50 or 100 cubic centimeter mark with soil not compacted, and weigh. Compute the amount of water-free soil in this.

$$\frac{(Volume\ of\ soil \times real\ specific\ gravity) - wt.\ of\ water\text{-}free\ soil}{Volume\ of\ soil \times real\ specific\ gravity}$$
$$= per\ cent\ of\ pore\ space.$$

What effect does size of particles have on total amount of pore space?

Does the amount of pore space increase or decrease with the amount of organic matter?

Which of the soils have the largest pores? Does this mean the greatest amount of pore space?

SECOND METHOD

Find what per cent the apparent specific gravity is of the real specific gravity, and subtract this from 100 per cent. The remainder expresses the per cent of pore space in the soil.

Why does the porosity of soils vary as the apparent specific gravity?

IX. — The Organic Matter in Soils

The common sources of the organic matter in soils are plants and animals whose bodies, after life leaves them, fall to the ground and are gradually disintegrated and mingled with the finely ground portions of the earth's crust.   Here, through the action of soil bacteria, the particles are decomposed into the elements from which they were originally formed, and thus their cycle of existence is completed.

In the intermediate stages of decomposition this organic matter in the soil is called *humus*, and is a most important factor in the matter of the soil's producing power.

Humus is the chief source of soil nitrogen.   Its presence in the soil usually imparts to it the dark color which is regarded as one of the surest indications of a fertile soil.   Many of the most important physical properties essential to the permanent productiveness of soils are dependent upon the presence of a certain proportion of organic matter mixed with the rock particles.

In Exercise 12 the student is given a method of determining with some degree of accuracy the per cent of organic matter in any given sample of soil.   Ignition is not regarded as an altogether satisfactory means of taking this measure, because the heat that consumes the organic matter also drives off any volatile salts and water of hydration present, thus indicating by the loss of weight in the ignited soil a greater amount of organic matter than the soil may have contained. This is especially true in the case of clay subsoils. However, with most surface soils the results are approximately correct and are of value in making comparisons between different soils.

REFERENCES : King, *The Soil*, pp. 94–95. Fletcher, *Soils*, pp. 53, 72, 322–333. Snyder, *Soils and Fertilizers*, pp. 86–96.

EXERCISE 12

Determination by Ignition of the Loss of Organic Matter by Cropping

It is a recognized fact that constant cropping with grain tends to diminish rapidly the amount of organic matter in the soil unless great care is taken to maintain the supply by the use of green manure crops or the application of farmyard manure. This loss changes the physical character of the soil. The result is to destroy granulation, lessen the water-holding capacity of the soil, lower the temperature, and interfere with proper aëration.

Get one sample of the surface soil from a field that has been cropped heavily for years, and another sample from the sod border as near as possible to this field, and determine the loss in weight of each soil on ignition, which will give an indication of the organic matter content.

Weigh out 5 grams of water-free soil, or air-dry soil calculated to a water-free basis, and ignite in a small crucible to low red heat for 15 to 20 minutes. Cool in a desiccator and weigh.

Tabulate your results.

Which of the soils loses more ? Why ?

X. — The Water-retaining Power of Soils

The capacity of a soil to absorb or hold water is limited by the amount of its total pore space, which, as is shown in previous paragraphs, varies according to the composition and texture of the soil from about 25 per cent to more than 50 per cent. This means that a saturated soil may contain from 436 tons to 697 tons of water in the upper foot of soil on an acre.

However, a productive soil is never saturated with water except possibly for a short time immediately after a long and heavy rainfall. Soils in which water stands for any length of time filling the pore spaces are boggy and unproductive, and the water-table must be lowered by artificial drainage before the lands can be valuable for farming purposes.

But it is the power of drained soils to retain moisture, which is of real interest to the farmer, for this is the water supply on which the growing crops must depend.

It has been stated in a former paragraph that the moisture which is retained in a soil is held there in the form of a film around each soil particle, and is known as capillary moisture. Hence, it is readily seen that the soil which possesses in any given volume the greatest surface area in the grains which compose it has the greatest water-retaining capacity. For this reason the finest-grained soils have the greatest power to retain moisture. This is illustrated as follows: In a cubical box measuring 12 inches, only one ball having a diameter of 12 inches can be placed. The surface of this ball, by the formula for finding the surface of a sphere ($S = \pi D^2$), equals 144 π inches. If balls of half this diameter be placed in the box, it will contain eight of them, and their combined surfaces ($S = \pi \times 6 \times 6 \times 8$) are 288 π inches. That is, by reducing the diameters of the spheres by one half, the aggregate area of their surfaces is doubled.

While the soil particles composing any soil are not perfect spheres and are not of uniform size, it still holds that the finer the grains and the greater the number of them in a given volume of soil the greater will be the internal surface of the soil and the greater its water-retaining power.

Exercise 13, therefore, is a practical demonstration of the differences in the capacities of soils to retain moisture largely in accordance with the relative sizes of their soil particles.

REFERENCES : King, *The Soil*, pp. 157–162. Fletcher, *Soils*, pp. 80–82. Warington, *Physical Properties of Soil*, pp. 74–85.

EXERCISE 13

Power of Soils to retain Water

Fill tubes having perforated bottoms with sand, silt, loam, and clay.

Before filling, place disks of damp cheese cloth in the bottoms of the tubes and then weigh them. Fill the tubes up to the crease, one inch from the top, by pouring the soil in gently through a funnel, the tube being held vertically, and be careful not to compact the soil by jarring. Weigh the filled tubes and place in an empty galvanized iron box.   Pour water into the box till it is on the same level with the soil in the tubes, thus allowing the water to pass up through the soils.   Note time required for soils to become moist on top.   When the soils have become thoroughly saturated, remove the tubes and place them in a pan to drain.   Weigh from day to day till drainage ceases.

Determine the amount of water-free soil by finding total moisture content of the soil when used.

Measure depth of the settled soils.

Calculate the per cent of water retained, the weight per cubic foot of soil that this represents, using the apparent specific gravity and the acre inches of water.

Express your results in tabular form.

Land recently plowed six inches deep will absorb how many inches of rainfall without any run-off?

Is there any advantage in deep plowing on rolling land?

What is a saturated soil?

XI. — Effect of compacting the Soil

There is some difference of opinion among farmers as to whether rolling or otherwise compacting the soil increases its capacity to retain moisture.   It is frequently apparent that the soil on the surface of the ground where it has been packed by footprints has more moisture than the loose soil around it.   It is true that, by pressing more closely together the grains of loose material on the surface and destroying the open spaces which were too large to exert capillary action, the movement of water from below towards the surface has been increased, and for a time there will be a gain in the amount of water in the upper layer of the soil, but at the expense of the layers below. In the case of some very light soils, where the particles in their composition are quite uniformly coarse and the pore spaces large, compacting undoubtedly increases their water-retaining power.

Exercise 14 is given for the purpose of comparing compact soils with loose soils to determine which has the greater capacity to retain water.

REFERENCES : King, *The Soil*, pp. 200–202. Fletcher, *Soils*, pp. 171–177.

EXERCISE 14

Power of Compact Soils to retain Water

Use the same tubes and soils as in Exercise 13, and run them at the same time if possible. When you have filled the tubes one-third full of soil, hold them vertically six inches above a solid table, and let them fall three times ; repeat this when two-thirds full, and again when full. Use great care to compact the soil in all the tubes alike.[1]

Conduct the experiment precisely as in the previous exercise, except in compacting the soils. Calculate the per cent of water retained, the weight of water per cubic foot of soil, using the apparent specific gravity and the acre inches of water for each soil.

Tabulate your results.

[1] In the soil-physics laboratories of agricultural colleges an apparatus for compacting the soils uniformly is used. An iron plunger just fitting the soil tubes is attached to the end of a rod on which moves freely a weight of several pounds. The plunger is placed upon the soil in the tube and the weight dropped a given number of times from a mark on the rod. A strong wood frame is needed for the apparatus.

Which soil becomes wet on top first? Why? How does this correspond with total pore space? Which soil is drained first? Why? How does this correspond with total pore space? What effect does organic matter have on retention of water?

How does rolling affect the water-retaining capacity of a soil?

XII. — How Organic Matter in Soils affects their Water-holding Power

The chief object sought in the study of the science of agriculture is to discover how the farmer may control or modify to his advantage the conditions that affect the growing of crops. It is certain that crop yields are often seriously limited because the soil does not contain sufficient moisture to supply their needs.

Exercise 15 is given that the student may test the effect of an increase in the amount of organic matter in the soil upon its water-retaining powers.

REFERENCES: King, *The Soil*, pp. 288–291. Snyder, *Soils and Fertilizers*, pp. 37–38.

EXERCISE 15

Effect of Organic Matter on Retention of Water

Use same tubes as in preceding exercises, but compact in one, sand, and in the others, sand and peat in the following proportions: 190 grams of sand and 10 grams of peat thoroughly mixed; 175 grams of sand and 25 grams of peat; and 150 grams of sand and 50 grams of peat.[1]

[1] If peat cannot be obtained conveniently, thoroughly rotted dry manure may be used in its place. The manure should be made fine by rubbing before it is mixed with the sand.

Treat as in the preceding, and determine the grams of water retained, also the per cent of water retained, based upon the total amount of sand and peat used in each tube.

Tabulate results.

What per cent of organic matter was in each tube?

How many grams of water did the 10 grams of organic matter retain? The 25 grams? The 50 grams?

XIII. — Capillary Movement of Soil Moisture

As the films of moisture surrounding the soil grains which lie near the surface of the ground are removed by evaporation into the air, and others enfolding the particles of soil at greater depths are taken up by the tiny root hairs to supply the plants with water, there is a steady flow of moisture from below and from every side, if the soil is in a proper state of tilth, to take the place of that which has been withdrawn. This movement of moisture through the ground is made possible by the capillary action of soils, and in some soils its force is exerted through distances of many feet. If it were not for this capillary movement of moisture in soils, it would be utterly impossible in many regions to grow crops, since there is no rainfall there during the growing season. Indeed, there are few places where the rainfall is sufficient in quantity and distributed evenly enough during the months in which crops make their growth to meet their needs for moisture if none could be pumped up from the reservoirs below.

This power of a soil to move water through its mass is so largely dependent upon physical conditions which cultivation can affect that it should be one of the subjects of greatest interest and study for the farmer.

In Exercise 16 the students are able to observe the relative lifting powers of soils of different types and of soils of the same type but in different conditions of tilth.

The value of such ocular demonstrations to a student of the processes which are constantly in operation in the soil under his feet, and which it is possible for him to control, in a large measure, to the advantage of his crops, if he understands the principles on which these processes work, makes exercises of this sort especially desirable.

REFERENCES: King, *The Soil*, pp. 135–142. Fletcher, *Soils*, pp. 87–90, 95–96. Warington, *Physical Properties of Soil*, pp. 92–108.

EXERCISE 16

A Study of the Capillary Action of Soils

The capillary power of soils is influenced by several factors, the most important of these being the physical composition, texture, and compactness of the soil. In field soils all these are changed by continuous cropping, and the capillary action is therefore altered. Of these factors, physical composition is most important, especially the amount of the different grades of the inorganic constituents.

The soils selected are as follows : —
1. Fine sand.
2. Coarse sand.
3. Loam.

4. Clay.

5. Sod from an old pasture.

6. Heavily cropped soil as near the type of 5 as possible.

Use glass tubes one inch in diameter and four or five feet in length. One end of the large glass tubes is closed by means of a piece of muslin firmly tied on. These tubes are then filled with the finely pulverized and sifted air-dried soils. Great care must· be exercised in filling these tubes so as not to separate the coarse and fine particles. This may best be accomplished by holding the tube vertically during the process of filling. When the tubes are filled, the soil is compacted slightly by letting each tube drop four times a distance of four inches upon a book. The tubes are now placed in a supporting frame in such a manner that the ends shall dip one-half inch beneath the surface of the water contained in the tray.[1] The experiment is now ready for observation, and the datum to be obtained at each reading is the total height to which the water has risen. The readings are to be taken as nearly as possible at the intervals stated below and tabulated.

Observe height of moisture after $\frac{1}{2}$ hour, 1 hour, 2 hours, 3 hours, 6 hours, 9 hours, 12 hours, 24 hours, 36 hours, 48 hours; 3, 4, 5, 6, 7, and 8 days.

Make a close comparison of the different tubes.

Which shows the most rapid rise? Why?

Plot the heights of the water of the different tubes at different times.

At the end of one hour, which shows the greatest rise, clay or sand? Which at the end of a week? Why?

What effect does organic matter have, as shown in 5 and 6?

What effect does size of particles have on rapidity of capillary movement, not taking height into account?

[1] Arrange so that there shall be a continuous flow of water through the tray, keeping the depth half an inch above the bottoms of the tubes.

XIV. — A Common Mistake in applying Manure

Exercise 17 differs from No. 16 only in providing for experiments to determine the effect on the capillary movement of water caused by the application of farm manures or the plowing under of green crops.

The tests may easily be varied from time to time to cover a great many different conditions and to answer questions that may arise in the minds of the students as to what would be the results of certain practices.

If the crop at any time during its growing season is forced to depend for its moisture upon the supply of water which is held in store at some distance below the surface, any material, like coarse manure or unrotted clover, which breaks the connection of capillary tubes in the soil between the stratum where the plant roots are growing and the one in which the water is held will prove to be a serious disadvantage to the crop.

Experiments like the following are especially valuable, because they make clear to the student the reasons why certain ways of doing things on the farm frequently give bad results.

EXERCISE 17

Effect of Organic Matter on Rise of Water in Soils

Class exercise in which each member of the class is to take daily observations on the height of the water in the tubes and note effect of organic matter on rise of water.

After tying a cloth firmly over the ends of three two-inch glass tubes two feet long, fill them to the height of one foot with soil compacted by letting the tube drop four times on a book from height of four inches for every six inches of soil put into the tube.

Use finely pulverized, air-dried loam, filling tube No. 1 with the soil alone. Fill tube No. 2 with one foot of soil, then add a two-inch layer of cut straw or sawdust, and fill to the top with soil. Fill the third tube in the same way, except that a one-inch layer of fine, well-rotted manure is used in place of the straw or sawdust.

Place the tubes in a frame so that the lower ends shall stand in half an inch of water. Notice the rise of capillary water in each tube, and at the end of a week make a complete report of your observations.

What is the effect of plowing under large amounts of poorly rotted manure in the spring?

What advantage in this respect has fall plowing?

XV. — The Farmer's Control of Soil Moisture

The control of the moisture relations of soils includes : —

1. Increasing the amount of water in the soil either by irrigation or by rendering the surface more loose and porous, so that it will absorb a larger proportion of the water that falls upon it in the shape of rain and melting snows.

2. Diminishing the amount of water in the soil either by conducting it away through surface ditches before it soaks into the ground, or by tile drains laid beneath the surface for the purpose of lowering the water-table.

3. Increasing the water-holding capacity of the soil by cultivation and the application of organic matters.

4. Hastening or retarding the movements of water in the soil by different kinds of cultivation, or by the use of manures and green crops plowed under.

5. Conserving the supply of water that has already been taken into the soil, and preventing its unnecessary loss by evaporation from the surface.

All these questions except the last have been discussed in previous exercises. In Exercise 18 the object is to discover the most effective and satisfactory methods of conserving soil moisture by means of tillage.

In the study of the capillary movements of water it was seen that large amounts of moisture in many soils were being moved continuously from lower strata of soil to the upper zone to replace that which was being carried away in the atmosphere by evaporation. The water so removed is thus of no value to the crop, and is usually a serious loss. By destroying the capillary tubes that have formed close to the surface, the upward flow of moisture can be checked at this point and much loss of water be prevented. Frequent surface cultivation, for this reason, has been shown to be very effective in promoting the growth of crops in semiarid sections of the country and in all sections during protracted dry spells. The shallow stirring of the earth breaks up the capillary tubes that have formed in the compacted surface and spreads a loose blanket of dry earth — a dust mulch — over the surface.

Now in connection with this there are some questions that the farmer needs to have answered, such as : What depth of cultivation shows the best results in the conservation of moisture? How frequently should this cultivation be repeated to be most effective?

REFERENCES: King, *The Soil*, pp. 184–190. Fletcher, *Soils*, pp. 90–92, 107–110. Snyder, *Soils and Fertilizers*, p. 27.

EXERCISE 18

Effect of Soil Mulches on Evaporation of Water from Soils

Fill all the tubes, with the same kind of soil, compacting each [1] three inches, and pouring enough water upon it to make it thoroughly moist. Fill to within a half inch of the top, but do not pour water on the top. The enlarged bases of the tubes are then partially filled with water, and the tubes are left till the surface soil becomes moist. The tubes are then ready for use. As the water evaporates from the surface it must be replaced from day to day by refilling the base, the exact weight of water added in each case being noted.

The loss of water is determined by the loss in weight of the tubes. Weigh each day.

Tube 1, check (no cultivation).[2]

[1] The tubes used for this experiment are made of light galvanized iron, and are 18 inches long and 6 inches in diameter. The bases are 3 inches high and 8 inches in diameter. There is a rim round the top of the base, leaving an opening slightly larger than the tube. A collar is soldered around the tube $2\frac{3}{4}$ inches from one end, so that the tube, when standing in its base, rests on the collar, leaving $\frac{1}{4}$-inch space between the end of the tube and the bottom of the base. A small tube, closed with a cork, is soldered to the rim of the base, through which water can be supplied as needed.

[2] Cultivate the soil each morning with a knife to the depth indicated, being careful to lose none in the operation, as this would destroy the accuracy of the weights taken.

Tube 2, cultivated 1 inch deep.

Tube 3, cultivated 2 inches deep.

Tube 4, cultivated 3 inches deep.

Tube 5, cultivated 4 inches deep.

The cultivations should be made every day to the required depth. Each tube has an area of $\frac{1}{221850}$ of an acre, and the results are to be computed in tons of water evaporated per acre per week. It is very necessary that the tubes all have the same exposure to heat and air currents.

Upon what principle does a soil mulch conserve moisture?

What effect will cultivation have on a very wet soil?

If the water-table were 12 inches from the surface instead of 24, what difference would there be in your results?

Is there any argument in the experiment in favor of fall plowing?

Does it show the value of cultivating as soon as possible after a heavy rain?

XVI. — Mulches of Various Materials

For field crops of large areas the dust mulch secured by surface cultivation is probably the most practicable method of conserving soil moisture; but on more restricted areas devoted to orchards, small fruits, and gardens, it is possible to employ artificial mulches of manure, straw, leaves, clippings from the lawn, sawdust, peat, or sand. There are sometimes other advantages than the conservation of moisture secured in the use of these mulches; for instance, in the growing of some vegetables, such as potatoes, the protection of the roots and tubers from too intense heat seems to give good results. However, in Exercise 19 the thing to be determined is the relative effectiveness of artificial mulches of different materials.

REFERENCES: Fletcher, *Soils*, pp. 90–91. Snyder, *Soils and Fertilizers*, p. 35.

EXERCISE 19

Effect of Artificial Mulches upon Evaporation of Water from Soils

Fill tubes, as in preceding exercise, to within one inch of top, and then fill the remaining part with material for mulch. Proceed as in Exercise 18.

Tube 1, check (filled to top with same kind of soil).

Tube 2, one inch of sand.

Tube 3, one inch of gravel.

Tube 4, one inch of peat.

Tube 5, one inch of sawdust or cut straw.

The area of each tube is $\frac{1}{221850}$ acre.

Compute loss of water in tons per acre per week and tabulate results.

What will be the effect of these mulches on temperature?

What is the principle of the growing of "straw potatoes," *i.e.* covered with straw and not cultivated?

XVII. — Improvement of Heavy Soils by Use of Farm Manure

We speak of clays as *heavy* soils and sands as *light* soils, meaning not the relative weights of these soils, which is just the reverse of what the terms indicate, but that clays are plastic and sticky and difficult to handle when moist, while sands are loose and crumbly even when wet.

This characteristic of clay makes it a difficult and often unpleasant soil to cultivate, since one must exercise great care and judgment in not tilling it when it is too wet, and if it becomes too dry before working, it bakes so solidly that it can only be broken up into lumps; so that often no amount of labor can get the soil into good condition for cropping that season.

This undesirable quality in clays is due to the fineness of their particles, which allows them to pack too closely together. As was demonstrated in Exercise 6, the application of lime to such soils causes the fine particles to *flocculate* and form larger crumbs of material, which gives a looseness to the soil and helps to modify its plasticity.

Another way to treat clay soils to make them lighter and more porous in texture is to mix with the soil a dressing of manure, leaf mold, or some other form of organic matter.

The work in Exercise 20 is to demonstrate the beneficial effects of working organic matter into heavy clay soils, and to get some idea of the approximate amounts that should be used in order to change materially their character.

REFERENCES : Fletcher, *Soils*, pp. 322–327. Snyder, *Soils and Fertilizers*, pp. 93–96.

Exercise 20

The Effect of Organic Matter on Baking of Clay Soils

Use four one-gallon earthen jars provided with drainage outlets, and fill them to within one inch of the top as follows : —

No. 1. Clay.

No. 2. Clay thoroughly mixed with 5 per cent of peat by weight. (Fine, dry, well-rotted manure may be used.)

No. 3. Clay thoroughly mixed with 10 per cent of peat or manure by weight.

No. 4. Clay thoroughly mixed with 20 per cent of peat or manure by weight. Apply enough water to saturate the soil, using the same amount in each jar, and expose all the jars to the direct rays of the sun until the soil is baked.

Test the soils in the four jars to compare the ease with which the crust can be pulverized with the fingers.

Write out fully the results of this exercise.

What causes a clay soil to bake?

In what way does the crust thus formed injure growing plants?
How can a farmer prevent the baking of his soil?

PART II. — STUDIES ABOUT CROPS

XVIII. — What Foods Plants Use and How They are Obtained

IN the first twenty exercises of the *Manual* the study and experiments have had for their object a better understanding of the physical properties of the soil in its environmental relations to the plant.

The soil is called the home of the plant, inasmuch as it is its natural abiding place throughout its life, furnishing a spot for the anchorage of its roots, where they may find congenial surroundings as regards moisture, heat, and air, and a firm support from which to lift their aërial parts and expose the leaf surfaces to the air.

It is the business of the farmer to know what are the needs of the plant in these respects, and then how to manage his soil to secure in the fullest degree possible the conditions required.

But the important work of the plant is to *grow* — to take into its tissues certain substances that lie outside it, to transform these into its own substance, and to build them up into its various parts, thus enlarging and developing itself to its perfect stature and the completion of its life's functions.

What, then, are these substances which the plant uses for its building materials, and from what sources does it obtain them? These questions open up a new and broad field for the farmer's investigation.

Briefly stated, these are the answers that are now generally accepted for the above question: —

1. There are but ten elements which the plant requires for complete development of all its parts. These are carbon, oxygen, hydrogen, nitrogen, phosphorus, potassium, calcium, sulphur, magnesium, and iron. The symbols used to represent these elements, in the order in which they have been named, are C, O, H, N, P, K, Ca, S, Mg, and Fe.

There are two ways of determining the substances which plants require for the building of their parts. One way is to analyze the plants and so learn of what materials they have been made. In all plants analyses always show the presence of the ten elements that have been named. Usually a few other elements — silicon, chlorine, and sodium most frequently — are found present in the composition of the plants.

The second way is by synthesis — to grow plants either in distilled water or in pure sand, which insures that the growing plants get no plant food except what the grower gives to them and what they secure from the air. By this method it is demonstrated beyond all doubt that no plant can attain perfect development if not supplied with all of the ten elements, C, O, H, N, P, K, Ca, S, Mg, and Fe, and that the omission of any or all other substances in no way retards growth.

Moreover, in answer to the second question, as to the sources from which plants get their supplies of these essential foods, the investigations of scientists have shown that all the carbon and part of the oxygen used by the plant are taken from the air as the gaseous compound, *carbon dioxide* (CO_2), which enters the plant through minute openings in its leaves called *stomata*. The hydrogen and the remainder of the oxygen which the plant takes up are secured from the soil in the form of water, which is a compound of these two elements (H_2O). All substances which plants take up as foods — with the one exception, carbon dioxide — come from the soil and enter the plants through their roots in liquid form. That is, the hydrogen and oxygen are the elements of which the water is composed, and the nitrogen, phosphorus, potassium, calcium, sulphur, magnesium, and iron must all exist in the soil as soluble compounds, — solids like salt and sugar that dissolve more or less readily in the water in the soil, — and so the plants obtain them in solutions with the water absorbed by their roots.

This statement again emphasizes the lesson of so many previous exercises — the immense importance of an abundant supply of water for the crops, since water not only contains two of the essential plant foods, but is also the solvent and carrier of seven of the other eight. Six of these seven elements — phosphorus, potassium, calcium, sulphur, magnesium, and iron — are mineral compounds, locked up in the soil as constituents of the rocks. Nitrogen, however, is never found as an element in the composition of any of the rocks ; its source as plant food in the soil exists in the various organic compounds obtained from decaying animal and plant tissues — the humus of the soil.

Since nearly four fifths of the atmosphere is free nitrogen, it was first thought that plants secured their nitrogen, as they do their carbon, directly from the air. But this was long ago disproved, though the belief continued that the ultimate source of nitrogen in all organic compounds was the limitless supply of it in the air. This is now known to be true, and the claim has been made that no other discovery in the science of agriculture promises to yield results of such importance to the farmers as this : that there are certain forms of soil bacteria which have the power to take the free nitrogen directly from the air and build it into compounds that the plants can use.

Moreover, it has been discovered that these minute organisms make their homes and perform this work only on the roots of a certain kind of plants called legumes, which are best represented among our crops by the garden and field peas and beans, cowpeas, soy beans, the various kinds of clover and alfalfa. For each variety of leguminous plant there is a separate variety of bacteria which will live on the roots of this particular legume and on no other. (The one known exception to this statement is found in the case of the germs that live on the roots of alfalfa. These also thrive on sweet clover, which has been generally regarded as a weed.)

The presence of these bacteria in a soil is indicated by the little tubercles that grow on the roots of the legume that serves as the host plant for these organisms. These tubercles are the homes of colonies of the bacteria — millions of them in a single tubercle. The bacteria are thought to live on the juices of the plant's roots, and in return they furnish the plant with the nitrogen which they have the power to take from the air that permeates the soil about the roots of the plant. In this way the plant is not dependent for its nitrogen upon the supply in the soil, and when the crop is plowed under, or fed, and the manure returned to the field, an addition of this essential and expensive plant food is made to the soil without extra cost to the farmer.

Exercise 21 is the first of a number of exercises given in the *Manual* to teach some of the principles of soil fertility. The objects of this exercise are : —

(1) To show that nitrogen, phosphorus, and potassium are essential plant foods, and if the plant is deprived of any one of them it cannot complete its growth.

(2) To show the power of the nitrogen-gathering bacteria to supply the host plant with nitrogen taken from the air.

This experiment is believed to be one of the most valuable and practical exercises given in the course, and wherever a school can plan to conduct it, the classes should carry it through.

REFERENCES : Johnson, *How Crops Feed*, pp. 251–375. Johnson, *How Crops Grow*, pp. 126–220. Snyder, *Soils and Fertilizers*, pp. 57–229. Voorhees, *Fertilizers*, pp. 38–98.

EXERCISE 21

Soil Fertility

TO SHOW THAT CERTAIN PLANT FOODS ARE ESSENTIAL

Preparation of Pot Cultures

Use clean white sifted sand in 5-liter heavy glass battery jars, having 1 centimeter hole within 1 centimeter of the bottom. Into the hole fit a drain tube made of glass tubing with a glass-wool filter at the inner end, so that it will take liquid from the lowest place in the jar. Put up two series of eight of these pots.

To extract the sand, fill the jar within 1 centimeter of the top with dry sifted sand and add to this dilute sulphuric acid (made by adding 100 cubic centimeters of concentrated chemically pure sulphuric acid to 900 cubic centimeters of ammonia-free water) until the sand is saturated. Let stand two hours, and then add ammonia-free water, allowing the drainage to flow into a second jar until it is saturated. Allow this jar to stand two hours, and then wash both with ammonia-free water until free of acid, as shown by tests with litmus paper. In this way any soluble plant food is removed from the sand. One portion of acid extracts two jars. The sand for two of the jars, in which experiments are to be made to show the effect of nitrogen-gathering bacteria, is first heated to $120° - 130°$ C. for half an hour, and then extracted and washed as above.

Before planting, mix with the sand of each pot 10 grams of pure calcium carbonate to neutralize any possible acidity remaining.

In making applications of plant food, as indicated in the following table, and in such amounts as are there shown, the solutions to be applied to each pot are to be mixed together, and diluted to 1000 cubic centimeters. Mix thoroughly, and apply the whole amount to the pot, allowing any water present to be forced out through the drain.

The first application of the plant-food solutions is to be made at the time of planting, the second three weeks later, the third two weeks later, and subsequent applications at intervals of one week, each time as directed above.

Preparation of Plant-food Solutions [1]

Solution No. 1. Nitrogen: Dissolve 80 grams of ammonium nitrate in 2500 cubic centimeters of distilled water. [2] Use 10 cubic centimeters per pot.

Solution No. 2. Phosphorus: Dissolve 25 grams of monocalcium phosphate in 2500 cubic centimeters of ammonia-free water. Use 10 cubic centimeters per pot.

Solution No. 3. Potassium: Dissolve 50 grams of potassium sulphate in 2500 cubic centimeters of ammonia-free water. Use 10 cubic centimeters per pot.

Solution No. 4. Magnesium: Dissolve 20 grams of magnesium sulphate in 2500 cubic centimeters of ammonia-free water. Use 10 cubic centimeters per pot.

Solution No. 5. Iron: Dissolve 0.1 gram ferric chloride in 2500 cubic centimeters of ammonia-free water. Use 1 cubic centimeter per pot.

Prepare these solutions carefully, using chemically pure salts, and label each bottle.

For inoculating the sand in pot 8 with bacteria, obtain about a pound of soil from a field where there has recently been growing

[1] The instructor in chemistry should prepare these solutions for Exercise 21.

[2] If it is not convenient to prepare distilled water in a laboratory, *pure* rain water may be used in this experiment, both for washing the sand and watering the plants.

Pot No.	Preparation of Sand.	Plant Food Added.	Seeds Planted.
1	Extract and wash	None	Corn or Soy Beans
2	Extract and wash	All but N	Corn or Soy Beans
3	Extract and wash	All but P	Corn or Soy Beans
4	Extract and wash	All but K	Corn or Soy Beans
5	None	All	Corn or Soy Beans
6	None	All	Red Clover, Soy Beans, or Alfalfa
7	Heat, extract, and wash	All but N	Red Clover, Soy Beans, or Alfalfa
8	Heat, extract, and wash	All but N Bacteria	Red Clover, Soy Beans, or Alfalfa

the same legume which is to be used in this experiment, being sure that tubercles were present on the roots.   Put this soil in a glass fruit jar and shake thoroughly with about one quart of pure water.   Then let settle, and as each seed is planted add 10 cubic centimeters of the clear liquid before covering the seed.

Why is $CaCO_3$ added?   Why are two of the pots heated?

Observe each week, and make observations about differences of growth and appearance.

Thin the corn and bean plants to three in each pot and the clover plants and alfalfa to ten.

The pots should stand where the heat and light conditions are favorable for rapid growth, and where all conditions except those controlled in the application of plant-food solutions are the same for every plant.

XIX. — Farming in Four-gallon Pots

In Exercise 21 the plants were grown in glass battery jars filled with sand from which all plant food had been extracted. In this way complete control of the food conditions is secured in studying the effects of the omission of any particular element, because it was known exactly what foods were furnished for the plant and what was lacking.

Notice that in the experiments the tests are confined to the elements nitrogen, phosphorus, and potassium. The reason is that these are the only plant-food elements about which the farmer usually needs to concern himself. The supply of carbon dioxide in the air, though it constitutes not more than 6 parts in 10,000 of the atmosphere, is always sufficient to meet the needs of the crop for carbon and oxygen, and the question that demands the attention of the farmer here is only that of preserving an abundant and healthy leaf surface for his growing crops.

From the water contained in the soil the hydrogen, and more oxygen, are obtained. Sulphur, magnesium, and iron are used by plants in small amounts as compared with the other foods, and most soils contain enough of them to meet crop requirements for thousands of years. The demand for calcium as a plant food is not large, but many soils are more or less acid, and these need applications of lime to correct this condition.

In the case of nitrogen and phosphorus, however, and to a less degree in Illinois, of potassium, the amounts of these elements which are removed from the soil in large crops, as compared with the amounts shown by analyses to be contained in the surface foot of most of these soils, are so great that maintaining a sufficient supply of some or all of these three elements in the soils to make possible the raising of maximum crops for any number of years becomes a serious problem in soil fertility.

In the pot-culture work of Exercise 22 regular field soils are used, the object being to test the needs of the soils selected for whatever crop is being grown in respect to the three plant foods, — N, P, and K.

The amounts of the fertilizers used in each pot are carefully computed on the basis of the amounts of each element, which are removed from an acre by maximum crops, *i.e.* 100 bushels of corn, 100 bushels of oats, 50 bushels of wheat, etc.

Pots 1, 5, and 10 are used as checks for the purpose of comparison. The difference between the yield of pot 2 and the average of the yields of pots 1, 5, and 10 will indicate the soil's need of nitrogen. In the same way the question is asked in pot 3 for phosphorus and in pot 4 for potassium.

It may happen that there is a deficiency of plant food in two elements, or even three, and in this case there can be no material increase in the yields until all the food requirements of the crop are met. These points will be settled by the tests made in pots 6, 7, 8, and 9.

A regular plant house or conservatory is, of course, the best place for pot-culture work, but these exercises can be used wherever house plants can be grown. One thing is very essential — all pots must be given exactly the same treatment as to soil, moisture, heat, light, and planting, the only condition in which there is a difference being the application of plant food.

REFERENCES: Johnson, *How Crops Feed*, pp. 251–375. Johnson, *How Crops Grow*, pp. 126–220. Snyder, *Soils and Fertilizers*, pp. 57–229. Voorhees, *Fertilizers*, pp. 38–98.

EXERCISE 22

Applications of Plant Food for Crop Production

Use four-gallon earthenware pots in series of ten pots for each crop. The pots should have holes in the bottoms for drainage. Fill another pot of smaller diameter, heaping it full of sand, and turn over this the pot in which you wish to make a hole, so that the bottom on the inside rests on the sand. Then with a sharp punch and a few light blows of a hammer a hole can be easily made.

Fill the ten pots of each series with the same soil, taking it from the field which you wish to test for the crop you are going to grow, as oats, barley, wheat, red clover, alfalfa, sugar beets, or any of the garden crops.

In collecting the soil for the pots, take it from the upper seven inches, which is about the depth of the usual plow line.[1]

Apply the plant foods according to directions given below : —

1. None (check).
2. Nitrogen.

[1] To make the conditions follow more closely field conditions, two collections of soil should be made as follows: Remove the soil which is to be used in the experiment to the depth of 7 inches and place it in a box. Then put into a second box the soil underlying this in the stratum from 7 to 12 inches below the surface. In filling the pots, use soil from the second box for the bottom, and on 5 inches of this place the surface soil from the first box.

.   Phosphorus.
    Potassium.
    None (check).
    Nitrogen, phosphorus.
    Nitrogen, potassium.
8. Phosphorus, potassium.
9. Nitrogen, phosphorus, potassium.
10. None (check).

For applications of nitrogen, use $\frac{1}{2}$ ounce (16 grams) of dried blood per pot; for phosphorus, use $\frac{1}{4}$ ounce (8 grams) of steamed bone meal; for potassium, use $\frac{1}{8}$ ounce (4 grams) of potassium chloride. Mix the plant food thoroughly with the soil in the pots to the depth of 7 inches, a few days before the seeds are to be planted.

The pots used in these exercises are $10\frac{1}{2}$ inches in diameter and $11\frac{1}{2}$ inches deep (inside measurements). This gives a surface area for each pot of about $\frac{1}{7260}$ of an acre, so that one gram application of plant food, or every gram of yield of crop, corresponds to one pound per square rod, or 160 pounds per acre.

XX. — Experiment-field Work for High Schools

The University of Illinois Experiment Station now has twenty-three experiment fields distributed over all parts of the state. Each year interest in the work done on these fields has increased, not alone among those directly engaged in farming, but among all classes of people who are beginning to recognize their educative value.

Within the past year a number of high schools have been provided with land to be used in teaching agriculture. These school fields generally range in size from five to ten acres. In some cases the land has been given to the school, in others it has been bought or rented by the district, and in still other cases a landowner interested in having agriculture taught in the school has donated the use of as much land as the school needs for the purpose.

Dr. C. G. Hopkins, Professor of Agronomy, University of Illinois, and Chief of Agronomy of the Agricultural Experiment Station, offers to assist any schools in the state that wish to establish experiment plots in the laying out of their plots and the planning of the work to be done on them.

Already two or three high schools have availed themselves of this offer, and their fields have been plotted for school work. There is reason to believe that popular sentiment favoring this branch of school work is so strong that it will not be difficult for any high school to secure enough land to establish an experiment field to be used in connection with its courses in agriculture.

This work with the plots does not duplicate the pot-culture work given in Exercise 22, though each may be regarded, in a way, as a complement of the other.

In the work with the pots certain tests may be made that require a more complete control of conditions than can be secured in field work. On the other hand, in the experiments on the plots, the crops are grown under the natural conditions with which the farmer deals, and on a scale sufficiently large to make it possible to compare results with those on the surrounding farms. If the work is carefully planned in the beginning, and then the plans are followed and the results obtained each year are kept as a permanent record, the experiment plots will every year increase in interest and usefulness as a part of the school work in agriculture.

The outlines of the work given in Exercises 22 and 23 were prepared by Dr. Hopkins, and were published in a leaflet a few years ago. Exercise 21 is taken from *Laboratory Manual for Soil Fertility*, by Dr. Hopkins and Professor J. H. Pettit, where it is given as Practices 16 and 17.

REFERENCES : Johnson, *How Crops Feed*, pp. 251–375. Johnson, *How Crops Grow*, pp. 126–220. Snyder, *Soils and Fertilizers*, pp. 57–229. Voorhees, *Fertilizers*, pp. 38–98.

EXERCISE 23

Plot-culture Tests to Determine the Plant Food Requirements of the Soil

The size of the plots to be used will be determined by the amount of land available for this work.

Where the area is restricted, the plots may be laid off in rectangles $\frac{1}{2}$ rod by 2 rods and separated from each other by sunken paths not less than 2 feet wide. This will give each plot an area of one square rod ($\frac{1}{160}$ of an acre). If the school possesses more land, larger plots up to tenth acres (2 rods wide and 16 rods long), with half-rod strips separating them, may be laid off, as is done on the experimental fields at the University.

The plant-food applications for the smaller plots (one square rod), to be made annually, are as follows : —

Plot No. 1. None (check).

Plot No. 2. Nitrogen.

Plot No. 3. Phosphorus.
Plot No. 4. Potassium.
Plot No. 5. None (check).
Plot No. 6. Nitrogen, phosphorus.
Plot No. 7. Nitrogen, potassium.
Plot No. 8. Phosphorus, potassium.
Plot No. 9. Nitrogen, phosphorus, potassium.
Plot No. 10. None (check).

Apply the nitrogen in the form of dried blood, 16 pounds per square rod ; phosphorus as steamed bone meal, 8 pounds per square rod ; potassium as potassium chlorid, 4 pounds per square rod. The plant foods should be well worked into the soil to the depth of about 7 inches a few days before planting, care being taken not to mix the soils from adjacent plots.

Several different field and garden crops should be planted in rows across all of the ten plots.   Oats, barley, wheat, clover, alfalfa, etc., can be planted in rows 8 inches apart, dropping the seeds about 1 inch apart in the row ; radishes, lettuce, carrots, beets, peas, etc., in rows 16 inches apart ; sweet corn, potatoes, cowpeas, soy beans, etc., in rows 32 inches apart ; field corn in rows 40 inches apart ; and cucumbers and melons 64 inches apart.

A marker with five runners 16 inches apart is easily made of boards, and it will serve to mark good straight rows across all of the plots for all crops.

By this system of planting every crop will be represented on every plot, and the effect of all of the different kinds of soil treatment can be noted on each crop.

If the complete experiment cannot be undertaken, a fairly satisfactory experiment can be made by using only the first five pots or plots.

In planning these soil-fertility experiments, it is well to bear in mind that very sandy soil is likely to be most deficient in nitrogen.

In ordinary Illinois soil, especially that which has been under cultivation for many years with clover in rotations, the element phosphorus is most deficient. In peaty soils, potassium is most deficient.

In drawing conclusions from results which may be obtained in these experiments, it should be understood that while we may apply purchased nitrogen in order to obtain information quickly as to the needs of the soil, the nitrogen should be obtained in all general farming by the slower process of growing leguminous crops which, when provided with the proper bacteria, can get nitrogen from the air.

The three plant-food elements, nitrogen, phosphorus, and potassium, are contained in most soils in rather small amounts. Indeed, it often happens that the soil furnishes so little of one or more of these elements that the plant suffers for that kind of food. In such cases we can grow larger crops by giving the plant the food it needs.

To find what elements of plant food are most deficient in the soil, we should experiment and see what effect is produced on the growth of plants by adding different plant-food elements to the soil.

For nitrogen, dried blood should be applied. This contains from 12 to 14 per cent of nitrogen in a form which is not likely to injure the plant, even if used in some excess. A 100-pound bag of ground dried blood can be obtained from Swift & Company, Union Stock Yards, Chicago, for about $2.50.

For phosphorus, steamed bone meal should be applied. The best steamed bone meal contains from 12 to 14 per cent of the element phosphorus in a very good form for plants. A 100-pound bag of extra fine ground steamed bone meal (" Big Six " brand) can be obtained from Morris & Company, Union Stock Yards, Chicago, for about $1.25.

For potassium, use potassium chlorid. This is a salt which usually contains from 40 to 42 per cent of the element potassium. A 100-pound bag of potassium chlorid can be obtained from Armour Fertilizer Works, Union Stock Yards, Chicago, for about $2.50.

The Armour Fertilizer Works, Union Stock Yards, Chicago, have agreed to furnish a one-pound package of potassium chlorid, a two-pound package of fine ground steamed bone meal, and a four-pound package of ground dried blood for a total charge of seventy-five cents, the purchaser to pay express charges.

These quantities are ample for pot-culture experiments.

XXI. — Questions relating to the Seeding of Crops

There is found among farmers to-day a great difference of opinion — or a great indefiniteness of opinion — about the quantity of seed per acre in the various crops that should be sown to give best results. In the case of oats, for instance, is it better to make a thin seeding to encourage the tendency of the plants to tiller, or will heavier yields of better quality of grain be secured by planting so thickly that each seed will produce but a single stalk and head? There are as strong adherents to the one practice as to the other.

It may be that experimental work on such subjects by school classes in agriculture will add little to the sum of knowledge which we already have about it; but it is by becoming interested in work of this kind that men are trained to think independently and to form definite opinions, supported by scientific principles and personal experience. Such work as is given in Exercises 24 and

25 has been found very profitable in the agricultural schools in Canada.

The work is not at all difficult for a class to handle, but it will require care and thought. The seed should first be tested to determine its vitality. The pupils will find that some samples of oats will contain very many more grains in a bushel than others. This raises other questions for them to consider. For example : — Shall more or less seed be sown on fertile soil than on one that contains less plant food ? Such problems concern alike the farmer and the student.

REFERENCE : Hunt, *The Cereals in America*, p. 302.

EXERCISE 24

Crop Production: Oats

To Determine what Amount of Seed per Acre gives Best Results

On a series of 10 plots of one square rod each, in which all conditions are similar, except the amount of seed used, make seedings of oats as follows : —

Plot 1. Sow $3\frac{1}{5}$ ounces (rate of 1 bushel per acre).
Plot 2. Sow $4\frac{1}{5}$ ounces (rate of $1\frac{1}{2}$ bushels per acre).
Plot 3. Sow $4\frac{4}{5}$ ounces (rate of 2 bushels per acre).
Plot 4. Sow   8 ounces (rate of $2\frac{1}{2}$ bushels per acre).
Plot 5. Sow $9\frac{3}{5}$ ounces (rate of 3 bushels per acre).
Plot 6. Sow $11\frac{1}{5}$ ounces (rate of $3\frac{1}{2}$ bushels per acre).
Plot 7. Sow $12\frac{4}{5}$ ounces (rate of 4 bushels per acre).
Plot 8. Sow $14\frac{2}{5}$ ounces (rate of $4\frac{1}{2}$ bushels per acre).
Plot 9. Sow 16 ounces (rate of 5 bushels per acre).

Make the drills 8 inches apart and cover $1\frac{1}{2}$ to 2 inches deep. During the season of growth observe the differences in the tendency of the plants to "stool" due to thickness of planting.

When ripe, harvest each plot separately and thresh with a flail. Weigh and record the yields of each plot, giving their acre equivalents.

XXII. — Methods of Sowing Grains

Another question relating to the growing of oats and other spring grains, which still remains unsettled in the minds of many farmers, is whether drilling or broadcasting is the better way to sow the seeds. The one method insures a more perfect covering of the seed at a uniform depth; the other may give a more even distribution of the grain over the whole surface at less cost for labor and machinery. It is a good experiment for classes in agriculture to work on. Of course, the results of a single season cannot settle the matter. There are so many conditions that affect the growing of a crop which are seasonal, and differ from year to year, that it will require the results of many tests to give any reliable basis on which to form conclusions; but if these experiments were continued in a school year after year, and the records were taken accurately and left for succeeding classes to use and extend, it is certain the work could be made worth while.

REFERENCES: Hunt, *The Cereals in America*, pp. 131, 296, 304. Dondlinger, *The Book of Wheat*, pp. 65–69.

Exercise 25

Crop Production: Oats

Test of Drilling *versus* Broadcasting

Lay off four plots of one square rod each and prepare them all for seeding in the same way, then sow oats as follows :—

Plot 1. Sow $4\frac{4}{5}$ ounces ($1\frac{1}{2}$ bushels per acre) in drills 8 inches apart and cover $1\frac{1}{2}$–2 inches deep.

Plot 2. Sow $4\frac{4}{5}$ ounces ($1\frac{1}{2}$ bushels per acre) broadcast and cover with a garden rake.

Plot 3. Sow $6\frac{2}{5}$ ounces (2 bushels per acre) in drills 8 inches apart and cover $1\frac{1}{2}$–2 inches deep.

Plot 4. Sow $6\frac{2}{5}$ ounces (2 bushels per acre) broadcast and cover with a garden rake.

Observe differences in growth between the oats drilled and those sown broadcast.

Harvest and thresh crops on each plot separately and record the yields, giving results in acre equivalents. Write conclusions.

XXIII. — Special Treatment of Seed

The farmer who would succeed in the work of growing crops must not only know how to prepare and treat the soil, how to breed and select seed, how to plant the seed and cultivate the crop, but he must also know how to protect the growing plants from the many forms of insect enemies and fungus diseases which seem to be increasing from year to year in numbers and destructiveness.

A disease which is very common in oat fields and much more serious in its effects upon the yield of the crop than most farmers realize is smut. There are two forms of this disease : loose smut, which attacks the whole head and turns it into a black mass of spores; and closed smut, which affects only the kernels, and is not so easily seen.

If the farmer were helpless in combating this enemy, it might be well to let him remain ignorant of the amount of the loss it causes him. Professor Zavitz, of the Ontario Agricultural College, who has conducted experiments for many years in growing and improving oats, says that in many fields the loss from smut amounts to 40 per cent or more. A few years ago a careful investigation of the oat fields of Wisconsin was made through the assistance of graduates of the College of Agriculture, and it was found that 17 per cent of the crop that year was destroyed by smut.

And yet there are two simple and inexpensive treatments by which this disease can be completely prevented. It is the purpose of Exercise 26 to familiarize the students with these methods of treating the seed which are now known to be effective in safeguarding the crop from smut. There would be an increase to the country annually of millions of bushels of oats if the farmers could be taught to use one of them.

Since the spores of the fungi which cause the smut in oats are attached to the seed and develop in the growing stem of the plant until the head appears and is ready for their attack upon it, any treatment of the seed which will kill these spores and not injure the vitality of the grain for seed purposes will be effective, and two such treatments are given for practice in Exercise 26.

Students will be impressed with the extent and seriousness of this disease if they make inspections of oat fields to determine the per cent of the crop that is affected by it. Let each student provide himself with a lath frame having an area of one square foot. In different parts of the field in which the examination is being made, place this frame on the ground, count the numbers of stems of oats inclosed by the sides of the frame, and also the number of stems bearing heads affected by smut. In this way, by finding the average of the fractions showing the proportion of diseased heads to sound ones, a fairly accurate determination of the per cent of loss in this oat crop caused by smut can be made.

On fields or plots where treated seed is used, leave a narrow strip for comparison, and here sow untreated seed. Then find the per cents of diseased heads of oats where the two kinds of seeds were used. A comparison of these records should be conclusive proof of the value of treating seed oats for smut.

Exercise 26

Treating Seed Oats for Smut
First Method

On a tight floor spread a few bushels of the seed to be treated. Make a solution of concentrated formalin (a forty per cent solution of formaldehyde), using one pint of the formalin to forty gallons of water. Apply this solution to the oats with an ordinary sprinkling pot, wetting the top of the pile, then stirring the grain with a shovel and continuing the sprinkling and stirring until every kernel is thoroughly moistened. Now shovel the grain into a pile and cover with a blanket or sacks for about 12 hours to prevent too rapid evaporation of the formalin.

Then uncover and shovel the pile over two or three times, and the seed will be dry enough to sow.

The price of formalin is from sixty to eighty cents a pint, and the treatment of the seed will cost from two to four cents a bushel.

Second Method

Have two vessels — large tubs or barrels are best — and fill them nearly full of hot water. Let the water in one vessel be at a temperature of 110°–120° F., and in the other 132°–133° F. Have near at hand a bucket of cold water and a kettle of boiling water to use in keeping the liquid in the large vessels at the required temperatures.

Put a bushel of oats in a sack and dip it into the water at 110°–120° F. Leave it a minute for the mass to become warmed through, then change it to the other vessel of water at 132°–133° F. Keep a thermometer in the water, and should the temperature rise or fall, control it by adding cold or hot water, as may be needed.

Every two or three minutes raise the sack of grain out of the water and lower it again. This will aid to saturate the whole mass thoroughly.

Keep the seed in the hot water for ten minutes, then spread out on a floor and dry sufficiently for sowing. Repeat with as many bushels as are needed. Each of these methods of treating the seed for smut, if the work is done thoroughly, will kill all the pores and completely protect the crop from this disease.

XXIV. — Studies with Corn

In many ways corn is much the most satisfactory of all crops for class study and experiment work. It is planted and makes considerable growth in the spring before the close of the school year, and its season is so long that it is still standing and maturing its grain when school work begins again in the fall.

Being planted in open rows, it is easy of access for observation and experiment work. Cultivation plays a larger part in the growing of corn than it does with our other important cereals, and for this reason the success of the crop is more dependent upon the care it receives during the growing season than in the case of the other grains.

Moreover, it is the greatest wealth-producing crop in the United States; and hence especial attention is being given to the improvement, selection, and care of seed and to methods of cultivation.

The structure of the plant also lends interest to its study. The fact that the stamens, which are the pollen-bearing organs of the corn plant, are produced on the top part of the stalk, — the tassel, — while the pistils, the other essential organs of the flower, — in corn called the silk, — are where the ear is borne makes it possible for the corn breeder to control the matter of inbreeding and self-fertilization and to a large degree determine the parentage of each kernel of corn.

In the case of corn, as with oats, wheat, and other small grains, there is much uncertainty of opinion as to the proper thickness of planting and width of rows. Many experiment stations are working on this problem, and the results of their tests will be published later. Probably the particular value that work such as that outlined in Exercise 27 will have in school agriculture will come from directing attention to the importance of the farmer's having some definite knowledge on such questions as a guide to farm practices, and in the training that it gives to those who are to manage farms and who should know how to settle these problems for themselves. These are matters that directly affect the profits of farming; and it is good training to teach the pupils that agriculture is a business full of problems to be settled, and that those who make it a success must know how to handle them.

In considering the thickness of planting and the best distance between the hills, try to determine whether it is largely a question of sufficient supply of plant food in the soil, a more even distribution of corn roots through the whole area covered, or the best exposure of the plants to sunlight and air.

REFERENCE : Hunt, *The Cereals in America*, pp. 227–234.

EXERCISE 27

Crop Production: Corn

TO DETERMINE HOW CLOSE TO PLANT CORN

Prepare five plots of one square rod each for corn, making the conditions alike for all plots; then plant as follows : —

Plot 1. Hills 4 feet × 3 feet, 4 stalks in a hill.

Plot 2. Hills 4 feet × 1 foot, 1 stalk in a hill.

Plot 3. Hills $3\frac{1}{3}$ feet × $3\frac{1}{3}$ feet, 3 stalks in a hill.

Plot 4. Hills 3 feet × 3 feet, 3 stalks in a hill.

Plot 5. Hills 3 feet × 3 feet, 2 stalks in a hill.

Before planting, the seed should be carefully tested for germination, and on plots (1), (3), (4) plant five grains, and a few days after the corn is through the ground, thin to the required number. On plots (2) and (5) plant three grains, and thin as required.

When the corn is mature, husk and weigh, giving the yields of each plot reduced to acre equivalents.

XXV. — Problems in Cultivating Corn

In growing corn it is an almost universal practice to cultivate the soil between the hills, from the time the plants are through the ground so that the rows can be seen until they are too large to permit a team to be used, and then in many cases some cultivation is done later by hand with the hoe.

The method of cultivation employed to-day and the implements that are used in cultivating corn now differ widely from those of a generation ago ; but in those days, as at the present time, a large factor in the cost of growing the crop was in the tillage that was believed to be necessary while the corn was growing.

Considering the importance of this item of expense, and the fact that the sort of cultivation that was once practiced in corn growing is now almost wholly discarded, we may well consider what is the real purpose of the work given to the cultivation of corn and what would result if some or all of this work were omitted.

In Exercise 28 the difference in the treatments of plots 1 and 3 is to see whether the early preparation of the soil, as in plot 1, will result in storing a larger supply of water in the soil to the advantage of the crop so as to make it profitable to apply this extra labor.

In plot 2, compared with 1, and plot 4, compared with 3, the test is made to see whether the frequent cultivations usually given to the corn field are valuable because they destroy the weeds or because they stir the surface soil.

And the treatment of plot 5, when the results are compared with those of plots 3 and 4, should show whether it is very important to keep the weeds from growing with the crop.

This work should be repeated each year, recording the results together with the special weather conditions of the season. If a number of schools in the country carry on the same experiment, there will be increased interest and value in the results obtained.

REFERENCES: Hunt, *The Cereals in America*, pp. 218–225. Orange Judd Co., *The Book of Corn*, pp. 87–95, 115–127, 167–191.

EXERCISE 28

Crop Production: Corn

To show Effects of Different Methods of Tillage

Use 5 plots of one square rod each ($\frac{1}{2}$ rod × 2 rods), planting on each plot 3 rows of corn, running lengthwise of the plots, 3 feet apart, the hills being 3½ feet apart in the row, 3 stalks to each hill.

Prepare the soil for planting as follows : —

Plot 1. Plow (or spade) as early in the spring as the soil is in condition to work, and thoroughly cultivate the surface each week until the time of planting.   Keep the plot free from weeds, and a loose surface mulch until the ground is thoroughly shaded by the corn.

Plot 2.   Prepare the ground for planting as in plot 1, but after the corn is planted do not stir the ground at all.   Keep the weeds down by shaving them off with a sharp hoe.

Plot 3.   Do not plow (or spade) the ground until just before planting.   Then cultivate the plot through the season carefully, as in the case of plot 1.

Plot 4.   Do not prepare the ground until ready for planting. After planting, treat the plot in the same way as was done with plot 2, merely shaving off the weeds at the surface.

Plot 5.   Prepare the ground for planting as was done for plots 3 and 4.   After planting, do nothing more, allowing the weeds to grow and the soil to remain packed and uncultivated.

During the season make notes from time to time of the appearance of the crops on each plot.   Take measurements of the height of plants and record them and other evidences of relative vigor of the crops on each plot.   Where were the signs of lack of sufficient moisture most apparent ?

At the proper season husk the corn on each plot, weigh and record the crops, reducing them to acre equivalents.

XXVI. — How Moisture may be saved for the Corn Crop

It is the general belief that one of the chief benefits resulting to the crop from the frequent stirring of the surface of the soil is due to the conservation of the moisture content of the soil by means of the loose dust mulch.

The tests to be made in Exercise 29 are to determine how great are the differences in the amounts of water stored in the upper 40 inches of the soil due to the various cultural treatments that were used.

The differences in the amounts of water found on the several plots should be expressed in acre-inches and tons per acre.

REFERENCE: Hunt, *The Cereals in America*, pp. 235–242.

EXERCISE 29

Determination of the Water Content of the Soil on Each Plot for Exercise 28

Mark and weigh 30 soil pans, as in Exercises 2 and 3. (Run the determinations in duplicates.) Takes samples of surface, subsurface, and subsoil from each plot according to directions for Exercise 2. Weigh out 100 grams of soil in each pan, and let them dry at room temperature for a week. Weigh again, and the loss of weight will be the number of grams of capillary moisture contained in the soil. A comparison of the amounts of water found in the soils of the different plots will impress the value of tillage in the conservation of moisture.

Do the results show the value of preparing the ground for the crop as early as possible?

How much water has been stolen from the plots by the weeds?

XXVII. — Growth of Corn Roots

By far the greater part of the labor expended in growing the cereal crops is directed to bettering those conditions which affect the environment of the roots, and yet this is the part of the plant about which farmers generally have the most indefinite and incorrect conceptions.

The root naturally is the least conspicuous portion of the plant, and it is difficult to remove it from the soil without leaving behind so much of the delicate fibers and root hairs that one usually gets a very imperfect conception of the position which a plant's roots occupy in the soil and the extent of area that they cover.

To those who have not investigated this subject, it will be a surprise to learn how rapidly corn roots grow in a fertile soil and how soon they spread laterally to the center of the rows.

How deep the cultivation can safely be made between the rows of corn, and how close to the hill it is wise to stir the soil, even to the depth of two or three inches, are questions about which farmers differ.

Exercise 30 is given for the purpose of directing attention to a more thorough study of the root systems of plants and the habits of root growth, in order that the farmer may possess some reasonable basis for his decisions in the matter of the cultivation of his crops.

Such exercises as this will necessarily extend into the summer vacation ; but some pupils in some schools may become so interested that they will want to carry on the investigation during the summer and make their reports at the opening of the next year of school. In fact, an interest which will carry this work into the homes of the pupils and connect it with the work on the farm and in the garden must be the real test of the school's success in teaching agriculture.

REFERENCES : Hunt, *The Cereals in America*, pp. 336–340. Orange Judd Co., *The Book of Corn*, pp. 115–127.

EXERCISE 30

Crop Production : Corn

A STUDY OF CORN ROOTS.

Plant one plot of corn to be used for the purpose of investigations of the roots and the effects of deep and shallow cultivation.

Beginning one week after the corn appears above the ground, carefully remove a hill so as to preserve all the roots, wash the soil off, and examine the growth of the roots. How wide an area do they occupy in the ground ? How near the surface do they lie at 4 inches' distance from the hill ? How near the surface are they at distances of 6 inches and 12 inches from the hill ?

Once each week for the first six or eight weeks after planting, try to examine the roots of a hill of corn and take measurements of the spread and depth they have made, and their nearness to the surface at 4, 6, and 12 inches from the hill. This experiment requires considerable manual labor and patience to carry it through so that it shall have value. Each week it will be necessary to dig a deeper trench about the hill of corn and use more care to remove the soil without injuring the roots. However, it is of great importance to the corn growers to know how the roots of the corn plant develop and just how they lie beneath the surface.

To test the effects of deep cultivation, in which the roots of the corn plant are cut off, a simple tool can be made by fastening a handle to a solid block of wood about 6 inches square and 2 inches thick; then get a blacksmith to make a thin steel blade with three holes, so that it can be screwed to the block in such a way that it will project below two, four, or six inches, as desired. With this implement it is possible to run along the side of a row and prune the corn roots at any one of these three depths. A strip of lath fastened to the top of the block and extending to one side will keep the knife at the desired distance from the hill.

This pruning of the roots may also be done with a spade by tightly bolting two strips of wood on each side of the blade to serve as guards, and control the depth to which it can be thrust into the ground. By loosening the bolt at the ends of the strips, the guards may be raised or lowered.

Select a plot where the corn is of uniform growth. Lay off 8 rows, each containing 25 hills, and treat each row according to the following directions : —

Row 1. Shallow cultivation with a garden rake.

Row 2. Roots pruned 4 inches from hill and 2 inches deep.

Row 3. Roots pruned 4 inches from hill and 4 inches deep.

Row 4. Roots pruned 4 inches from hill and 6 inches deep.

Row 5. Roots pruned 8 inches from hill and 4 inches deep.

Row 6. Roots pruned 8 inches from hill and 6 inches deep.

Row 7. Shallow cultivation with garden rake.

The cultivation and pruning should be the same on all four sides of each hill.

The pruning should be done whenever the corn is cultivated, for the purpose of the experiment is to compare the results from deep and shallow cultivation in ordinary farm practice.

After each pruning of the roots, observe whether any of the rows wilt or show injury.

Take measurements of the growth in height of different rows. At husking time, harvest and weigh the corn from each row separately and record the results. Make a written statement of the conclusions reached by this experiment.

Exercise 31

Corn Breeding : Selection of Seed

The purpose of this exercise is to impress upon the minds of the students the fact that individual characters of plants are transmitted from parent to offspring, as in the case of animals ; and therefore, by selection of seed, the plant breeder may exercise large control in securing desired qualities in the crops that he raises.

Get permission from some farmer for the class in agriculture to go through his corn field in the early part of September and mark certain plants that show striking individual characters. For instance, find a corn plant that bears its ear very high on the stalk, and another plant equally vigorous that carries its ear lower than the average plants. Record the height of each ear.

Mark two other plants, one of which has two good ears, while the second has but one. Again, select a corn plant that is firmly rooted and stands erect ; and in contrast, a plant that is weak in its root and has fallen down. Also find a plant that shows a strong tendency to " sucker," and another free from suckers.

When the corn is fully mature, secure from the farmer the ears on the plants that you have marked, carefully number or label them, and record the special characteristic for which the plant was selected. Also select two ears from the crib of the same variety which have kernels of distinctly different types, one square in shape and the other rounded.

This will give ten ears for the experiment. Now, if possible, lay off a plot 2 rods × 5 rods, which will permit of 10 rows, each having 25 hills.   Plant each row from the seed of a single ear as follows : —

Row   1. Character : high ear.
Row   2. Character : low ear.
Row   3. Character : two ears to a stalk.
Row   4. Character : single ear to a stalk.
Row   5. Character : strong, erect stalk.
Row   6. Character : weak, prostrate stalk.
Row   7. Character : tendency to produce suckers.
Row   8. Character : free from suckers.
Row   9. Character : square-shaped kernels.
Row 10. Character : round-shaped kernels.

Give the same treatment to all the rows; observe during the season whether the plants of any of the rows show peculiarities of growth corresponding to the parent plant, and make a record of what you observe.

At the end of the season tabulate the results of the experiment as follows : —

Row 1. Average height of ears.
Row 2. Average height of ears.
Difference between the average heights of the high and the low ears.

Compare the average height of the high ears with height of the seed ear.

Compare the average height of the low ears with the height of the seed ear.

Row 3. What per cent of the plants have more than one ear?
Row 4. What per cent of the plants have more than one ear?
Row 5. What per cent of the plants stand erect?
Row 6. What per cent of the plants stand erect?
Row 7. What per cent of the plants have suckers?
Row 8. What per cent of the plants have suckers?

Row 9. What per cent of the ears have square kernels?
Row 10. What per cent of the ears have round kernels?

EXERCISE 32

Corn Breeding : Practice in Detasseling

Prepare a plot of ground (2 rods wide and of any length) for an experiment in corn breeding. This width of plot will allow for 10 rows, and the hills should be $3\frac{1}{2}$ feet apart in the row.

Use as seed the best ten ears of corn that you can get. Number the ears and the rows, and plant each row with seed from the ear of corresponding number. As soon as the tassels begin to appear, they should be removed from all the plants in every alternate row.

The work of detasseling is performed in this way : The tassels should not be cut off, as that is likely to injure the plant; but as soon as the tassel is sufficiently developed, and before the pollen is matured, a careful pull will separate it from the stalk at the top joint. It will be necessary to go over the plot several times to make sure that every tassel is removed from these rows before they ripen their pollen, for the tassels will not appear on every plant at the same time.

From the rows that are not detasseled remove all undesirable plants, *i.e.* (*a*) those that produce no ears; (*b*) those that show a tendency to grow suckers; (*c*) those that are weak in their roots; and (*d*) those that show any smut.

Seed ears are to be selected only from the detasseled rows, because with these plants there is absolute certainty that every kernel has been produced by cross-pollination.

This exercise is given mainly to furnish practice in the method that is generally followed now by breeders of pedigreed seed corn.

Harvest and weigh the corn from each row separately, and keep a record of results. If it is possible to continue this experiment from year to year, select the seed to be used the following year from the highest-yielding rows that were detasseled. Observe whether detasseling seems to increase or decrease the yield as compared with the rows bearing tassels.

EXERCISE 33

Experiment in Hand Pollination

In order to be certain in regard to both sire and dam in the production of seed, it is necessary to protect the pistils of the plants that are to bear the seed from any possible contact with the pollen grains of their own stamens or of those of any other plants except the ones chosen for the sires.

To do this in the case of corn, make a number of little bags of cotton cloth about 6 inches wide and 10 inches long. Narrow strips of the same cloth stitched in the middle to the edge of the mouth of the sack make convenient strings for holding the bags in place.

Before any of the silk appears on the tips of the young ears that have been selected for the dams, draw over each of the ears one of the cloth bags and tie it securely about the shank of the ear.

For mating with each dam, select the same number of corn plants to serve as sires, and as soon as the pollen on the tassels of these plants becomes mature and begins to shed, shake it off carefully from one of the plants into an open dish; now remove the sack from the ear of one of the dams and rub the ends of the silks carefully in the pollen that has been collected in the bottom of the dish, making sure that every one of the silks comes in contact with a grain of the pollen. Then replace the sack over the end of the ear, and do not remove it again until two or three weeks later.

To determine the difference in the vigor of seed produced by cross-pollination from that resulting from self-pollination (pistils fertilized by the pollen of the same plant), pollinate the silks of three or four ears with pollen taken from the tassels of the same plants. Mark the ears thus produced, and the following year plant a few rows with seed from these ears by the side of rows where cross-pollinated seed was used, and compare results.

Cross-pollinate the silk of an ear of white corn with the pollen from the tassel of yellow corn, and *vice versa*. What is the color of the cob grown on the stalk of white corn? What is the color of the grain on this ear? What is the color of the cob on the stalk of yellow corn? What is the color of the grain?

On one ear do not remove the sack nor apply pollen to the silk. After several weeks take off the sack, and notice how long the silk has grown. What does this teach?

XXVIII. — Observation Studies in the Cornfield

The development of the present breeds of cattle and other live stock plainly shows how careful, systematic, and intelligent selection has improved the animals. Plants respond to breeding and selection as readily as do animals, and there is no longer any doubt that varieties of corn may be further improved by similar methods. Experiments conducted by the Illinois Agricultural Experiment Station and other similar institutions have conclusively shown that the composition of the corn kernel may be varied at the will of the careful breeder ; that it is possible to increase or decrease the amount of oil, or of starch, or of protein by selection of seed.

It is equally true that greater variations may be made in the ears or the stalks by selection. The amount of husks, length of shank, size, and height of stalk, position of ear on the stalk, the number of leaves, and in fact every physical characteristic, can be varied in a short time by simple selection. It is just as important to know the character of every part of the corn plant as to know every characteristic of the animal. The size, shape, and characteristic of the stalk strongly influence the development of the ear and kernel of corn.

Get permission from a farmer whose land is convenient to the school to use his cornfield for the purpose of making a study of the corn crop. Have each pupil work on separate plots, ten hills square, and make his notes and records with reference to the following points : —

EXERCISE 34

Field Work with Corn

Name of variety_____ Size of field_____.

1. Date the corn matures : (*a*) roasting ear_____
(*b*) dented or glazed_____(*c*) ripe_____

2. Height of corn ; average of ten plants_____feet
_____inches_____

3. Total number of leaves on ten plants, taken from different hills
_____ Average number of leaves per plant_____

4. Total number of leaves below the ear on ten plants, taken from different hills_____ Average_____

5. Figure the total leaf surface on five average corn plants (for each leaf blade take twice the product of the length and average width) ------------

6. Length of ear stem, or shank (distance from joint, or node, to base of ear). Average of ten plants------------------

7. The ear stem, or shank, may be (1) *large,* — nearly or quite the diameter of the cob ; (2) *medium,* — or about half the diameter of the cob; (3) *small,* — or one third or less the diameter of the cob.

8. Husks : abundant, medium, scarce--------------

9. Husks : close, medium, loose-------------

10. Measure ten hills square ; give number of ears on these one hundred hills-------------- Average per hill------------

11. Give number of stalks in the above area having two or more ears--------

12. Give number of stalks in above area without ears (barren stalks) --------

13. Give average height of ears in above area--------------------------

14. Position of the ears on stalks : pointing upward ; horizontal ; pointing downward----------------------

15. Distance apart of hills each way---------------------------

16. Give number of hills per acre--------------- ------

17. Measure off one acre which represents a good average of the field ; husk one twentieth of this, and after weighing same carefully, estimate the average yield of field--------------------

18. If hills of corn are 3 feet 6 inches each way, how many hills to the acre ?--------------------

19. If, in a field of corn planted 3 feet 6 inches each way, there is on the average $1\frac{1}{2}$ pounds of corn to each hill, counting 80 pounds to the bushel to allow for shrinkage, what is the yield per acre ?--------

20. If corn is planted 3 feet 6 inches each way, and when mature is cut and put into shocks, each shock containing the corn from an area 14 hills square, how many shocks to the acre ?----------------------

How many of the shocks are 16 hills square ?--------------------

The following table will assist in making accurate estimate of the amount of land in different fields or plots : —

10 rods × 16 rods = 1 acre.	220 feet × 198 feet = 1 acre.
8 rods × 20 rods = 1 acre.	440 feet × 99 feet = 1 acre.
5 rods × 32 rods = 1 acre.	110 feet × 396 feet = 1 acre.
4 rods × 40 rods = 1 acre.	60 feet × 726 feet = 1 acre.
5 yards × 968 yards = 1 acre.	120 feet × 363 feet = 1 acre.
10 yards × 484 yards = 1 acre.	240 feet × 181.5 feet = 1 acre.
20 yards × 242 yards = 1 acre.	200 feet × 108.9 feet = $\frac{1}{2}$ acre.
40 yards × 121 yards = 1 acre.	100 feet × 145.2 feet = $\frac{1}{3}$ acre.
80 yards × 60$\frac{1}{2}$ yards = 1 acre.	100 feet × 108.9 feet = $\frac{1}{4}$ acre.

AREA OF ONE ACRE

10 square chains = 1 acre.
160 square rods   = 1 acre.
4,840 square yards = 1 acre.
43,560 square feet   = 1 acre.
640 acres = 1 square mile.
36 square miles (six miles square) = 1 township.

EXERCISE 35

Studies of an Ear of Corn

In order to become accustomed to the essential points in studying the characteristics of corn, the following suggestions are appended. Take ten ears each of two or more different varieties, preferably one yellow, one white, selecting ears as uniform and true to the variety type as possible. To get a close comparative study, it is advisable to lay all the samples on a table side by side. After studying the characteristics carefully, use this list for reference and bring out by example the points mentioned; then the work of scoring the samples may be taken up, following carefully the several points indicated on the corn score card as given on page 84 of this manual, and noting carefully the explanatory notes. Each sample of ten ears should be marked and known as "Exhibit A," "Exhibit B," etc. The letters (a) and (b), as used below, refer to the sample under examination, and it is intended that the corresponding characteristics possessed by each variety be marked in the blank space.

Name of variety (a)——————————(b)——————————

I. Color of grain : white ; yellow ; golden. (a)————(b)————

II. Color of cob: white ; light red ; dark red. (a)————(b)————

III. Surface of ear : smooth ; rough ; very rough. (a)——————
(b)——————————

IV. Rows of kernels : —

1. Are rows in distinct pairs (alternate spaces between rows of kernels wider than the others) ? (a)——————————(b)——————————

2. Number of rows (count three inches from butt). (a)——————
(b)——————————

3. Number of rows lost (disappearing after extending three inches or more from butt). (a)——————————(b)——————————

4. Spaces between rows : medium ; narrow ; wide. (a)——————
(b)——————————

5. Are rows straight (parallel with cob) ? (a)————(b)————

6. Are rows turned to the right or left (twisted to right or left of a straight line from butt to tip) ? (a)——————————(b)——————————

V. Grains on cob : dovetailed or mosaic-like ; firm ; loose ; very loose : (a)——————(b)——————————

VI. Shape of ears : —

1. Cylindrical (uniform in circumference from butt to tip). (a)
——————————(b)——————————

2. Partly cylindrical (uniform in circumference for a portion of length. (*a*)——————(*b*)—————

3. Slightly tapering (taper slight and regular). (*a*)—————

(*b*)—————

4. Distinctly tapering (taper very apparent). (*a*)—————

(*b*)—————

5. Very tapering (extremely tapering). (*a*)————(*b*)————

6. Are the ears in the exhibit too short or too long for their circumference ? (The proper proportion is for northern Illinois, 6.75–7.50 inches in circumference to 9–10 inches in length ; for central and southern Illinois, 7–7.75 inches in circumference to 10–11 inches in length). (*a*)————(*b*)—————

VII. Butts of ears : —

1. Even (entire end of cob exposed, with butt kernels at right angles to axis of cob). (*a*)—————(*b*)—————

2. Shallow rounded (cavity at butt shallow, broad). (*a*)—————

(*b*)—————

3. Moderately rounded (cavity moderately deep, medium diameter). (*a*)—————(*a*)—————

4. Well rounded (cavity at butt deep, small diameter where the shank is removed, rows of grains extending in regular order over the butt). (*a*)—————(*b*)—————

5. Compressed (cob rounded at end ; kernels at butt flat, smooth and short, indicating a tight husk). (*a*)—————(*b*)—————

6. Enlarged (large butt with no extra rows of kernels).

(*a*)————(*b*)—————

7. Expanded (large butt caused by extra rows of kernels).

(*a*)————(*b*)—————

VIII. Tips of ears : —

1. Kernels in rows (rows may be traced to tip). (*a*)——————

(*b*)——————

2. Flat (cob flattened at tip). (*a*)——————(*b*)——————

3. Filled (entire end of cob covered with kernels). (*a*)——————

(*b*)——————

4. Capped (a central kernel projecting from filled tip). (*a*)——————

(*b*)——————

IX. Kernels : —

1. Firm (rigid on cob). (*a*)——————(*b*)——————

2. Loose (movable on cob). (*a*)——————(*b*)——————

3. Upright (at right angles with surface of cob). (*a*)——————

(*b*)——————

4. Sloping (leaning toward tip.) (*a*)——————(*b*)——————

5. Square at top (corners not rounded at summit). (*a*)——————

(*b*)——————

6. Shoe-peg form (long, narrow kernel holding size to tip).

(*a*)——————(*b*)——————

7. Rounded corners (corners rounded at summit and base).

(*a*)——————(*b*)——————

8. Beaked (with long, sharp, tapering projection). (*a*)——————

(*b*)——————

X. Junction of ear stem, or shank, with ear: large; medium; small. (*a*)——————(*b*)——————

XI. Average length of ears : (*a*)——————(*b*)——————

XII. Average circumference of ears one-third distance from butt.

(*a*)——————(*b*)——————

XIII. Give ratio of circumference of average ear to length of average ear (divide length of ear by circumference of ear). [The proper proportion of circumference to length is as 3 to 4; or for medium varieties 7.5 to 10 inches.] (a)—————————(b)—————————

XIV. Weigh five ears from each sample, taking each alternate ear; give average weight of ears. (a)—————————(b)—————————

XV. Shell these five ears and give average weight of cobs. (a)—————————(b)—————————

XVI. Give average circumference of cobs one-third distance from butt. (a)—————————(b)—————————

XVII. Give ratio of circumference of average cob to average ear (divide circumference of ear by circumference of cob). (a)————————— (b)—————————

XVIII. Give percentage of grain: [Note.— To determine the percentage or proportion of grain to cob, select every alternate ear in the exhibit and weigh same. Shell and weigh the cobs; subtract the weight of the cobs from the total weight of the ears, giving weight of shelled corn. Divide the weight of shelled corn by the total weight of ears, which will give the per cent of grain. The per cent of grain should be from 86 to 90.] (a)—————————(b)—————————

XIX. Count the number of kernels of corn on the largest ear and on the smallest ear in each exhibit. (a)—————————(b)—————————

XXIX. — Judging and Scoring Corn

The object of corn judging, like that of stock judging, is to fix more clearly in the mind certain ideals of excellence which shall serve as standards of comparison to aid in the improvement of the products we are working to secure.

It is to the interest of the corn grower to produce the largest yields and the best quality of this grain at the greatest profit.

The careful study of corn has taught that certain characters of ear and kernel are closely associated with large yields and high quality. Taking these as the basis for a standard of perfection, the Illinois Corn Growers' Association has formulated a score card on which are indicated the several points to be considered in estimating the merits of a sample of corn and the relative degrees of importance of these points.

It has been found that the use of such a score card is a valuable aid to the judge or students in comparing and determining the relative merits of several samples of corn.

CORN SCORE CARD

Name of Scorer_____ Date_____

Post Office_____ Exhibit No._____

STANDARD MEASUREMENTS OF VARIETY

Name of Variety_____

Length_____

Circumference_____

Proportion of Grain to Cob_____

THE CORN SCORE CARD

The following is the score card of the Illinois Corn Growers' Association, as revised and adopted by that Association January 29, 1908. This should be used in judging varieties or samples not named, and also where the exhibit is not made under a variety classification.

Measurements for General Score Card

	Length. Inches.	Circumference. Inches.	Proportion of Corn to Cob.
Northern Illinois	9 – 10	6.75 – 7.50	88 per cent
Central and southern Illinois .	10 – 11	7.00 – 7.75	88 per cent

Points.	Perfect Score.	Score of Sample.
1. Uniformity of exhibit	5	. . .
2. Shape of ear	10	. . .
3. Length of ear	10	. . .
4. Circumference of ear	5	. . .
5. Tips of ear	5	. . .
6. Butts of ear	5	. . .
7. Kernel uniformity	5	. . .
8. Kernel shape	5	. . .
9. Color in grain and cob	10	. . .
10. Space between rows	5	. . .
11. Space between kernels at cob	5	. . .
12. Vitality or seed condition	10	. . .
13. Trueness to type	10	. . .
14. Proportion of shelled corn to cob	10	. . .
Total	100	. . .

Explanation of Points

1. Uniformity of exhibit : uniform in shape, length, and circumference.

2. Shape of ears : ears cylindrical, with straight rows and with proper proportion of length and circumference.

3. Length of ears : varies with variety measure.

4. Circumference of ears : varies with the variety measure.

5. [1]Tips of ears : oval shape and regularly filled out with large, dented kernels.

6. Butts of ears : kernels rounded over the end of the cob in regular manner, leaving a deep depression when shank is removed.

7. Kernel uniformity : kernels from the same ear and from the several ears uniform in size and shape.

8. Kernel shape : kernels deep, wedge-shaped, full at germ end.

9. Color : free from mixture and true to variety color.

10. Space between rows : furrow between rows and space caused by round corners of kernels, which should be narrow, deep, and sufficient for perfect ventilation.

11. Space between kernels at cob: space in row between kernels at cob.

12. Vitality or seed condition: ripe, sound, dry, and of strong vitality. Grains of a pinkish color objectionable. Three dead ears shall disqualify an entire exhibit.

13. Trueness to type: conforming to variety characteristics in variety classes, and to the prevailing type in general classes.

14. Proportion shelled corn to ear.

EXPLANATORY: How to study and apply the Points of the Score Card

Note A. — In all exhibits made prior to November 15 of each year, all standards of length and circumference shall be increased one-half inch, and standards of per cent shall be reduced two.

Note B. — The length and circumference of the general score card, for the northern district, shall be used in judging the standard varieties, when shown within that district of the state.

Note C. — Exhibitors may remove two kernels side by side from the same row at the middle of the ear for kernel examination.

1. The deficiency and excess in length of all ears shall be added together, and for every inch thus obtained, a cut of one point shall be made. Should the deficiency in length exceed ten inches, a cut of two points for each additional inch shall be made on the total score. In determining length, measure from the extreme tip to the extreme butt.

[1] It is recommended that judges interpret this rule very liberally, and that tips be not heavily cut for slight deficiency, so far as being filled over with kernel is concerned.

2. The deficiency and excess in circumference of all ears not conforming to the standard of the variety shall be added together, and for every inch thus obtained, a cut of one point shall be made. Measure the circumference at about one-third the distance from the butt to the tip of the ear.

3. In determining the proportion of corn to cob, weigh each alternate ear in the exhibit. Shell and weigh the cobs, and subtract from weight of ears, giving weight of corn. Divide the weight of corn by the total weight of ears, to get the per cent of corn. For each per cent short of the standard for the variety, a one-point cut shall be made.

4. In judging color, a red cob in white corn or a white cob in yellow corn shall be cut ten points. For one mixed kernel, a cut of one-fifth of a point shall be made ; for two, two-fifths of a point; for three, three-fifths of a point; for four, four-fifths of a point; for five or more, a, one-point cut shall be made. Kernels missing from the ear shall be counted as mixed, at the discretion of the judge. Difference in shade of color of grain or cob shall be scored according to variety characteristics.

MEASUREMENTS FOR NAMED VARIETIES

Certain varieties of corn have been grown and bred for a long time by men who by improved methods have developed certain characteristics of stalk and ear, such as color and shape of kernel, shape and size of ear, maturity, etc. Furthermore, each variety has its peculiar length, circumference, and proportion of corn to cob. Based on a careful study of the best samples of the different varieties recognized by the Illinois Corn Growers' Association, these variety standards are as follows : —

	LENGTH.	CIRCUMFERENCE.	PER CENT OF CORN TO COB.
Reid's Yellow Dent. . .	10 to 11 in.	7 to 7.75 in.	88
Leaming	10 to 11 in.	7 to 7.75 in.	88
Boone County White .	10 to 11 in.	7 to 7.75 in.	88
Riley's Favorite . . .	9 to 10 in.	6.75 to 7.5 in.	90
Golden Eagle	9 to 10 in.	7 to 7.75 in.	90
Silver Mine.	9 to 10 in.	6.75 to 7.5 in.	90
Champion White Pearl .	8 to 9 in.	6.75 to 7.5 in.	85

In judging corn, ten ears usually constitute an exhibit sample. It is desirable that samples be laid out side by side on a table where a good light may be had.

There is no better way to sort and select seed corn or to prepare a sample for exhibition than to place the ears from a bushel or so of selected corn upon a board or table, with the tips all pointing one way. Select the most perfect ear you can find, something which is your ideal type. Then, with this ear in your left hand, go over all the ears of corn upon the table, discarding those showing too great a variation from type in size, length, shape, roughness, and the size, shape, and indentation of kernel, etc.

. In preparing corn for exhibition, the ears should be groomed so as to present the best possible appearance by removing all husk, silks, and shanks, but do not mutilate or cut the ear itself in any way. Neither is it allowable to remove mixed kernels and substitute kernels of a proper color. The ears should be handled carefully, that no kernels be knocked off, for kernels that are missing are usually regarded as mixed, and the usual cut made for such imperfection. If the exhibit is to be sent away, each ear should be carefully wrapped in a piece of newspaper or other protection and firmly packed in a box.

NOTE A. — The score card cannot be used in absolutely mathematical sense. No set rules can be given ; it is largely a matter of the exercise of good sound judgment and patient practice on the part of the scorer. Where the number of points to be cut is not fixed by rules for judging, such as circumference, length, etc., the cut made should be in accordance to the degree of variance of each ear from value of the perfect ear, as fixed by standard.

REMARKS

As has been said before, the score card is intended to be largely suggestive. It is not an infallible guide, but is to be used rather as a staff, or cane, as it were, to help us and to give a little more intelligent direction as to the essential points to be observed in selecting corn either for seed or for exhibition purposes.

It should be borne in mind that while these ideal points and characteristics of the score card as described in the foregoing explanatory notes are desirable, other things being equal, the lack of perfection may not prevent a variety from producing high yields or having in other particulars desirable qualities. For example, the cob should be neither too large nor too small. It is evident that of two ears of equal size and compactness, the one with the small cob will have a deeper kernel and will contain more grain. On the other hand, while the small cobs may show a larger proportion of grain, yet the total weight of the ears may be much less and the yield per acre smaller. A large-sized cob is objectionable in that it usually carries a larger per cent of water, thus lowering the keeping quality of the grain and its vitality for seed.

In a well-proportioned ear the shelled corn will occupy about the same space as did the ear before it was shelled. It is a good relationship where the depth of grain is one half the diameter of the cob, or the circumference of the ear twice that of the cob.

EXERCISE 36

Testing Corn for Seed

The purpose in testing seeds is to determine, before planting, their vitality for germination and growth.

Several simple devices are used for this work, the essential things being an arrangement for keeping the seeds exposed to the proper conditions of moisture and heat, and the grains from each ear separate, so that a record of every ear tested may be kept.

The following method is recommended by the Agronomy Department at the University of Illinois : —

Have a tinsmith make a galvanized tray 16 inches square and 2 inches deep. Fill this tray with clean sawdust, thoroughly moistened before being placed in the tray, and pack it down firmly. If more convenient, use sand in place of sawdust. Cut a piece of white cotton cloth to fit inside the tray, and, with a ruler and good indelible pencil, mark it off into squares of $1\frac{1}{2}$ in. This will give 100 squares, and 100 ears of corn may be tested at a time.

Each square may be numbered, or the first square in each row. Have a pane of window glass of double thickness cut 15¾ inches square, so that it will fit rather loosely into the tray. The ears to be tested should be numbered. This may be done by tying a tag to each ear or pinning it to the butt.

When ready to fill the tester, take ear No. 1 in the left hand, and with the blade of a pocketknife pick out a kernel two inches from the butt. Lay this in square No. 1, germ side up.

Turn the ear one fourth round and take a second kernel two inches nearer the tip, placing this grain also in the first square. In the same way, turning the ear one quarter of its circumference and moving two inches nearer the tip each time, select kernels three and four, the last being taken two inches from the tip end. Lay them all in the first square with their germ sides up.

When the hundred squares are filled, each with four kernels, from ears numbered to correspond with the number of the square, lay the pane of glass carefully down on the grains so as not to move them from their places, and set the tray where the temperature will range during the twenty-four hours from 60° to 80° F. Such conditions can generally be found in the family living room or near the furnace in the cellar.

If the moist sawdust or sand is not packed into the tray until you are ready to place the grains in the tester, no more moisture will be needed. As the glass does not fit tightly in the tray, there will be sufficient access of air for the seeds.

Without removing the glass, it will be easy to see how the seeds are germinating. At the end of the sixth or seventh day, remove the glass and discard all kernels that have not put forth both a vigorous rootlet and a shoot an inch or more in length. No ear should be used for seed unless the four kernels germinate and show strong vitality. A class may work together on this exercise. Keep the records of all results.

CPSIA information can be obtained
at www.ICGtesting.com
Printed in the USA
BVHW071208201218
536078BV00015B/289/P

9 781330 874059